SNAP!

—

50 Creative Challenges for Aspiring Street Photographers

To Maria, for companionship, love and the picture on page 100.

SNAP!: 50 Creative Challenges for Aspiring Street Photographers
© 2024 Benke Carlsson & Dokument Press
ISBN 978-91-88369-94-9
GRAPHIC DESIGN Magnus Frederiksen
PRINTED Poland 2024

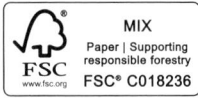

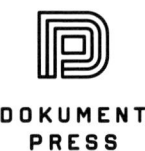

DOKUMENT PRESS

Årstavägen 26, 120 52 Årsta, Sweden
www.dokumentpress.com
hello@dokumentpress.com

BENKE CARLSSON

DOKUMENT PRESS

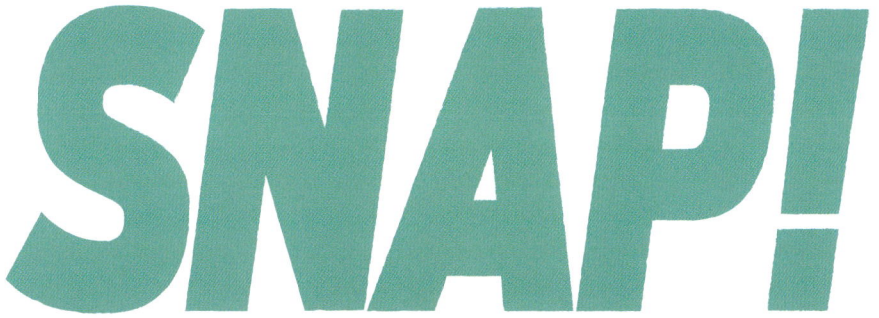

SNAP!

50 CREATIVE CHALLENGES FOR ASPIRING STREET PHOTOGRAPHERS

CONTENTS

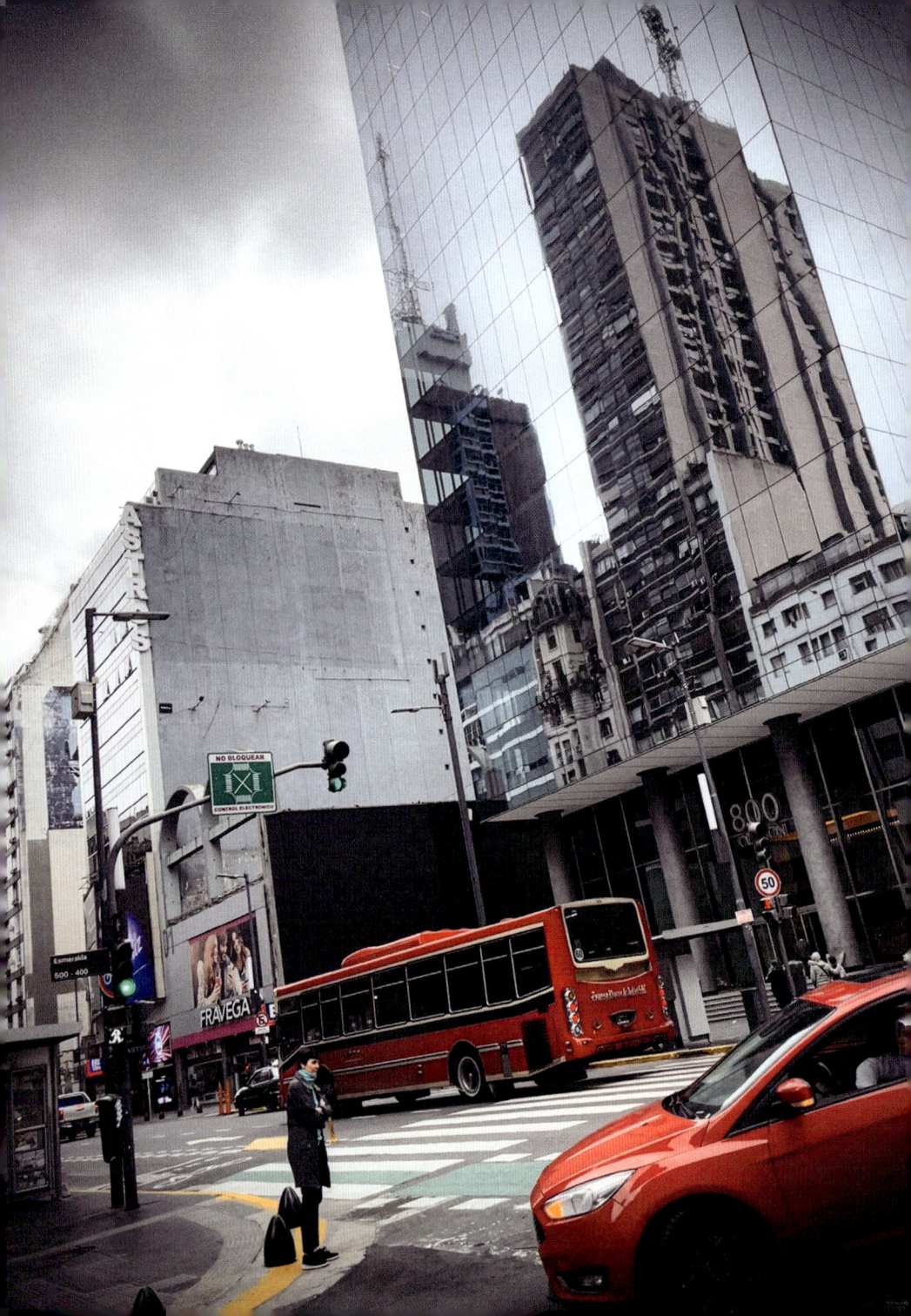

DRAMA WITHOUT A SCRIPT

OUR CITIES ARE full of visual stories. If you have the time and inclination, you can capture them. Most importantly, street photography is about taking in what goes on around you. It is an open-to-all activity that doesn't require any hi-tech camera or other equipment. My mobile phone works fine for me.

There is more street photography around today than ever before. The sheer output is astonishing, but you might wonder why so much of it looks the same. Street photographers are a motley crew. Some chase the magic moment, others social media likes. Where some seek photographic perfection, others simply want to look up from their phones and blend in with the crowd.

To me, it is a way of taking part in the theatre of the street. It may be a cliché, but behind every street corner you are confronted with a new scene where a detail, a gaze or an encounter becomes part of the show. Regardless of whether the drama is a comedy or a tragedy, the street photographer is an observer who captures everything from the ordinary to the spectacular.

IF YOU ARE OUT THERE SHOOTING, THINGS WILL HAPPEN FOR YOU. IF YOU'RE NOT OUT THERE, YOU WILL ONLY HEAR ABOUT IT.

Jay Maisel

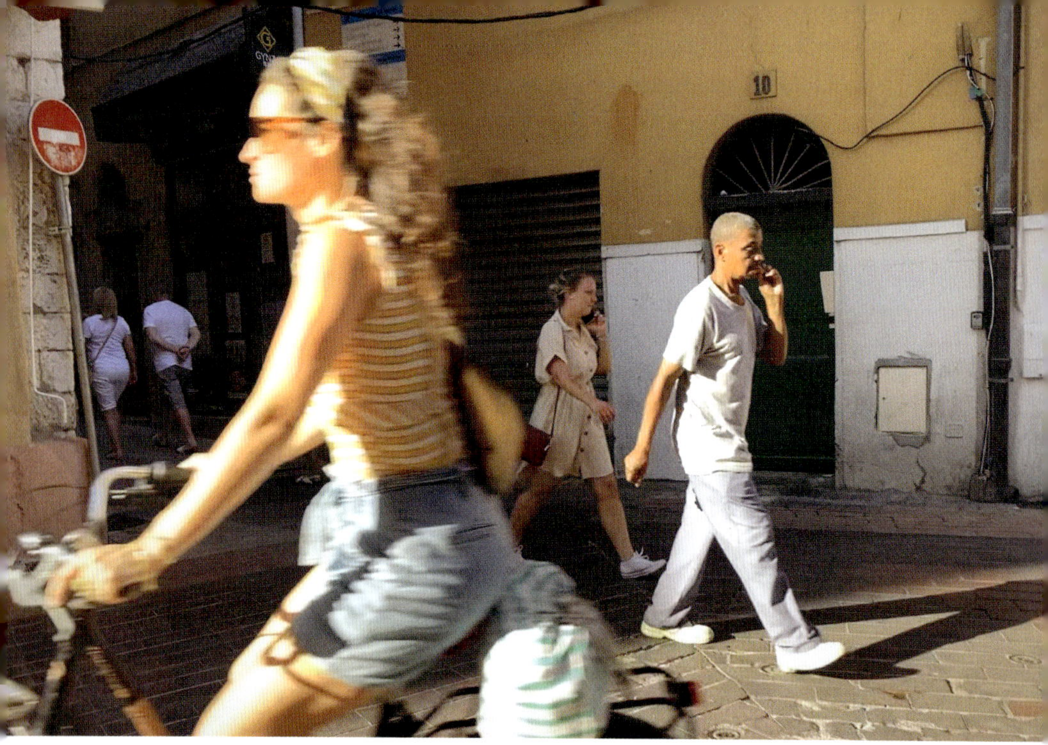
10
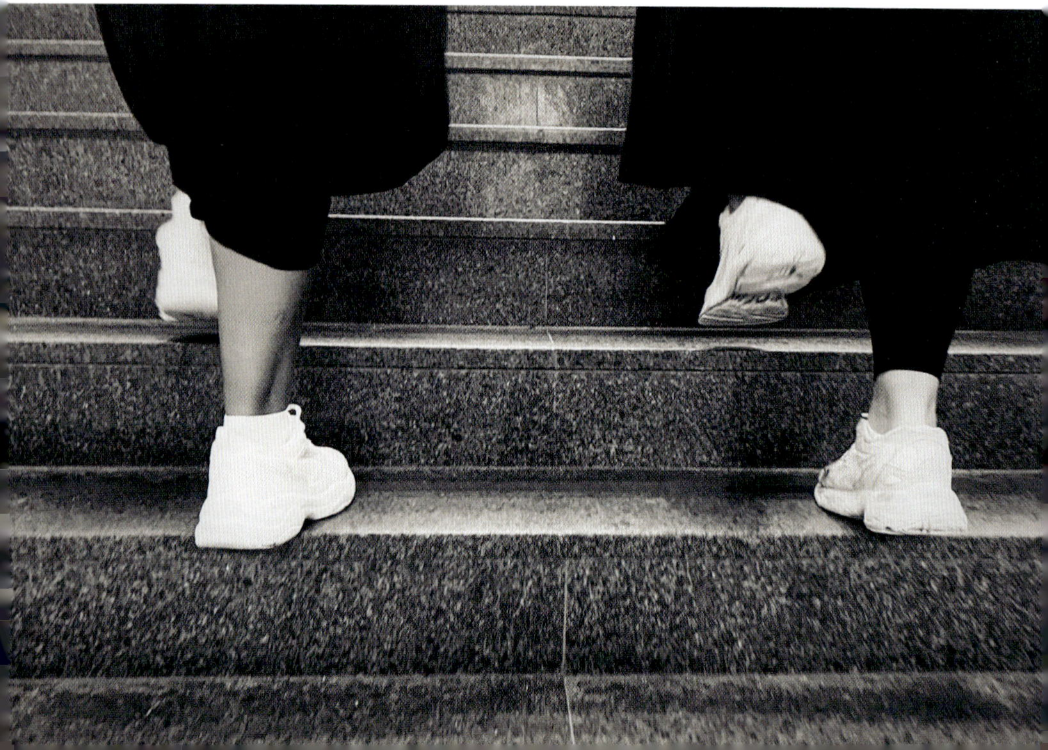

BEFORE YOU BEGIN

CURIOSITY. If there is a DNA of street photography, curiosity is a major element. If you enjoy exploring the city there are always new streets to venture down and new doors to open. There is practically no limit, and if you nurture your curiosity, you will continue to have a beginner's mindset, constantly looking for new paths, ideas and motifs. Let the camera feed your curiosity. Take a different path from the one you imagined.

THE CREATIVE ADULT IS THE CHILD WHO SURVIVED.
Ursula K. Le Guin

SPONTANEITY. The unexpected and the undirected are part of every street photographer's daily routine. Motifs appear when you least expect them to, just be prepared to act on them. It is all about the unexpected: a messy, grainy or out of focus image can be a natural part of the experience. Street photography is spontaneous, you can start whenever you feel like it. You do not have a set task or a deadline; you can experiment and develop your own style, at your own pace.

THE MARVELS OF DAILY LIFE ARE EXCITING;
NO MOVIE DIRECTOR CAN ARRANGE THE
UNEXPECTED THAT YOU FIND IN THE STREET.
Robert Doisneau

COURAGE. Many people find it challenging to approach strangers. Taking the picture of a stranger that may perceive you as a bit odd or pushy can be scary. But it is something you need to deal with, or many great pictures will never be taken. There is also a risk that taking photos becomes associated with feeling anxious or uncomfortable. You need to discover and push your limitations. You like people. You like to take pictures and you like to tell others why you do it. Be courageous!

*ONCE A WOMAN WHO DOES STREET WORK SAID TO ME,
'I'VE NEVER PHOTOGRAPHED ANYONE I HAVEN'T ASKED FIRST.
'I SAID TO HER, 'SUPPOSE CARTIER-BRESSON ASKED THE
MAN WHO JUMPED THE PUDDLE TO DO IT AGAIN
– IT NEVER WOULD HAVE BEEN THE SAME.
START STEALING!*

Imogen Cunningham

RESPECT. Curiosity, spontaneity and courage will get you far, but you need an additional dose of respect and restraint. It is easy to imagine that every picture needs to be taken, but how would you feel if a stranger photographed you? Some like it. Some are flattered. Others may get upset, scared or even angry. It can be difficult to know where the balance lies. These days, people are taking more pictures and having their picture taken more often, at the same time as they are getting more wary of its use. Some will wonder what you are up to. So be respectful and prepared to answer their questions. There are situations when a picture should not be taken – or when it should be erased.

*IT IS MORE IMPORTANT TO CLICK WITH PEOPLE
THAN TO CLICK THE SHUTTER.*

Alfred Eisenstaedt

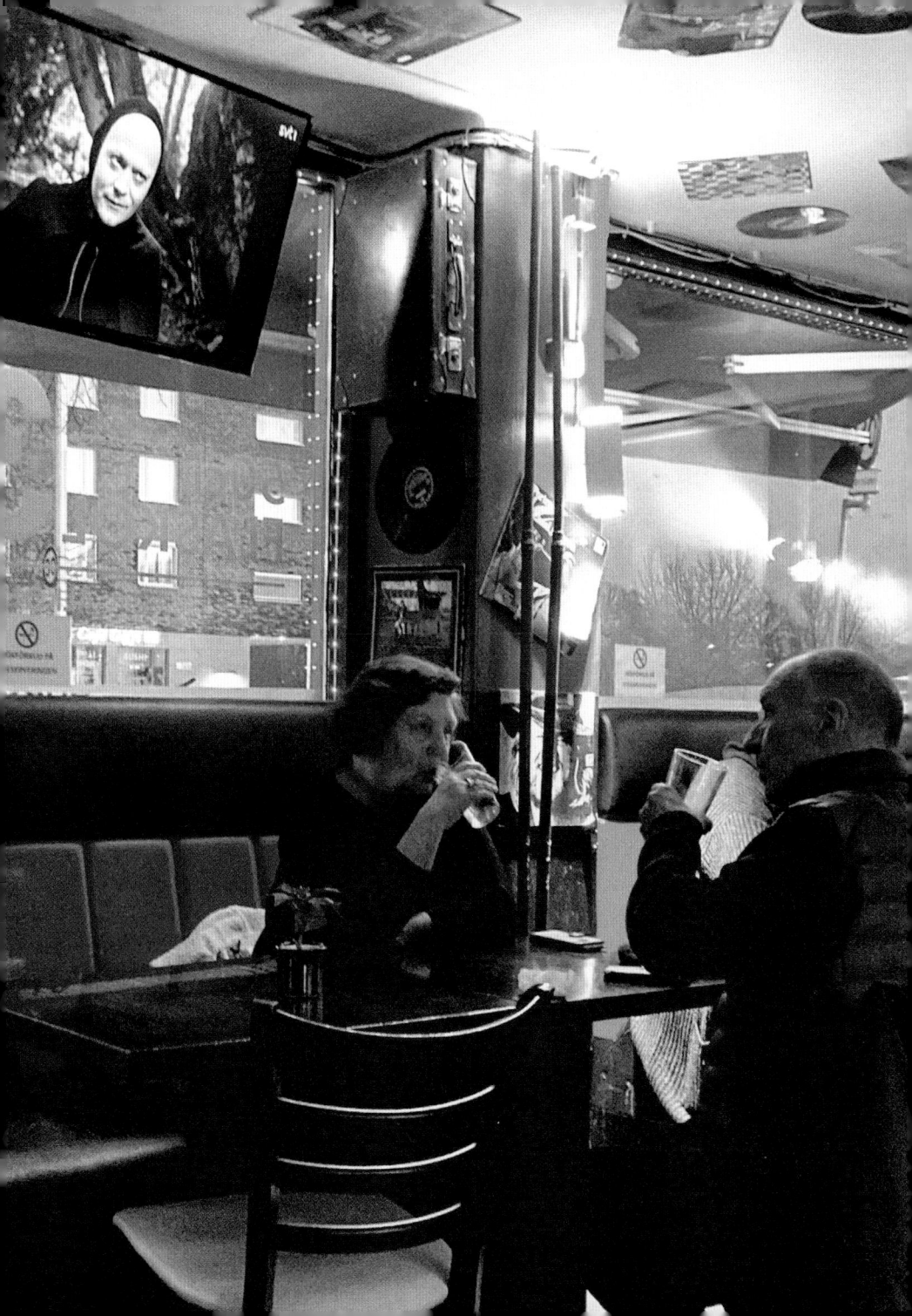

STYLE. Despite all the tips and guides – including this book – what you need to develop is your own style. It is about training your own gaze. Since there are many ways of doing it, you have to rely on trial and error. This requires commitment, patience, and time to experiment. Be inspired by others, read books, and look at a lot of photographs, and remember, it is when you begin to discover your own style that it really starts to get interesting. Let your experiences, values and personality influence your practice.

BE YOURSELF. I MUCH PREFER SEEING SOMETHING,
EVEN IF IT IS CLUMSY, THAT DOES NOT LOOK
LIKE SOMEBODY ELSE'S WORK.
William Klein

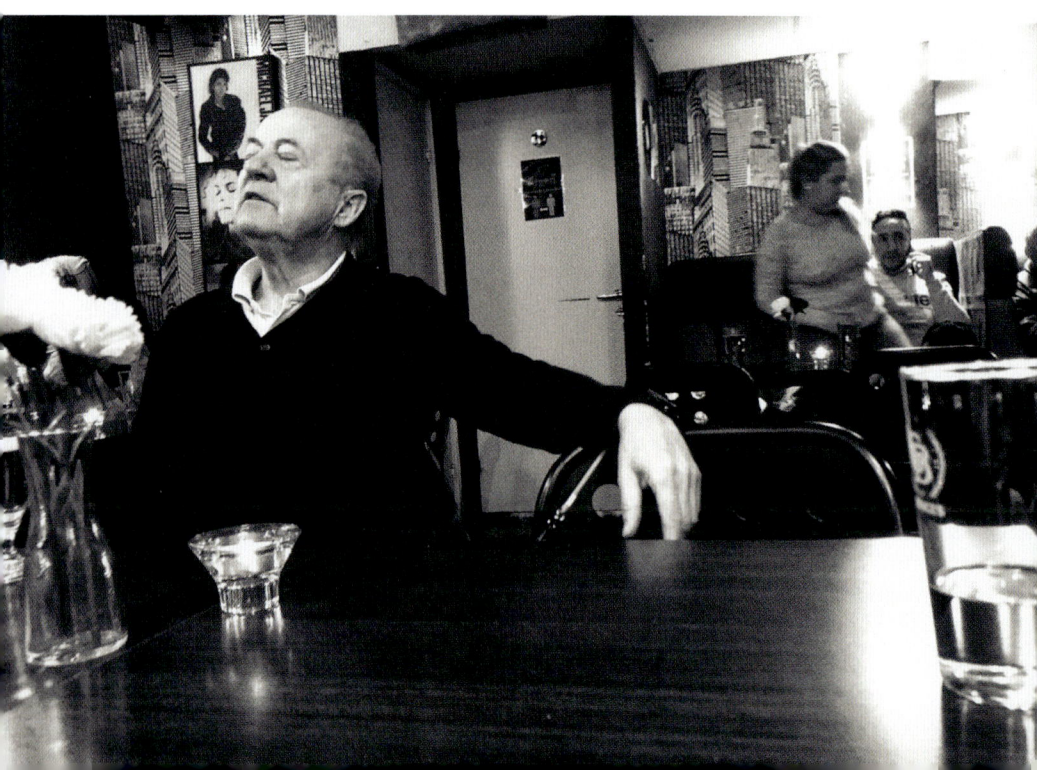

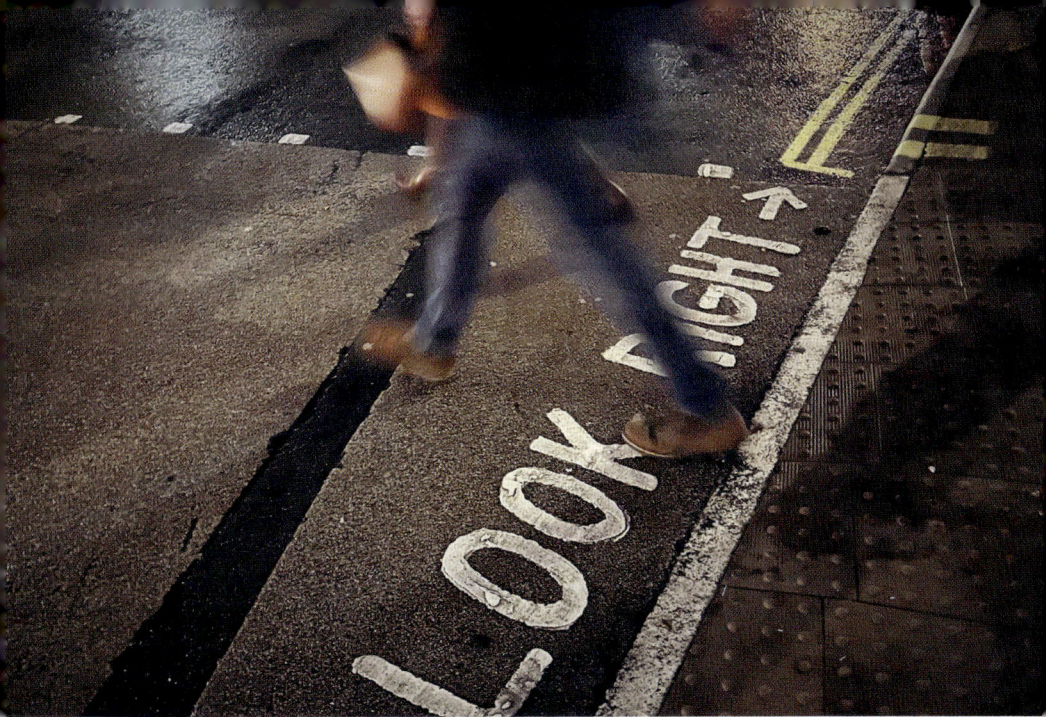

MISTAKES. It is okay if the picture is not straight, this happens frequently in street photography as you are often not in control of what's going on. Do not let it affect you. There are amazing photographers and projects to be inspired by, but becoming too careful, comparing yourself to others, or judging yourself too hard takes the joy out of it. Learn from your mistakes and hold on to that playfulness. Remember that the pros out there have worked long and hard, many of them as professional photographers.

STREET PHOTOGRAPHY IS 99.9 PERCENT ABOUT FAILURE. SO OFTEN I FEEL DEFEATED BY THE STREET. I SOMETIMES FIND, HOWEVER, THAT IF I KEEP WALKING, KEEP LOOKING, AND KEEP PUSHING MYSELF, EVENTUALLY SOMETHING INTERESTING WILL HAPPEN.
Alex Webb

RIGHTS AND OBLIGATIONS. The laws and regulations that apply to cities and towns can differ, and it is important that you are aware of them. Photography in public spaces is generally permitted, even when people do not know they are included. You can generally photograph what you want, but when you are not on your home turf, make sure you know the rules. Remember there is a great difference between taking a picture and how you use it. There is a difference between private and commercial purposes. If you are taking a picture for commercial purposes you need the subject(s) consent. It is a good idea to know the difference between legal restrictions, which are binding, and ethical limitations, which are about what is right and fair. When you photograph children, or people in a vulnerable situation, you need to think twice. If you are photographing at a private property: a flat, a toilet or a changing room, your conduct could be considered inappropriate. You should always be aware of what is considered private and what is not, and if you happen to find yourself, for example, at or near a military installation. Photography may be forbidden in shopping centres or on private property. To conclude: it is okay to take pictures, but you need to be aware of the rules and regulations and be able to explain what is appropriate to others, who may have their own ideas of right and wrong.

INSPIRATION. Whether you are aware of it or not, the way you experience the city is influenced by advertising, media, art, etcetera. Adding to your stock of impressions and knowledge will have a bearing on your choice of motif. Read books, watch movies, and study other people's photographs. When it comes to street photography, saying that we have moved from sparsity to abundance in only a few decades is hardly an exaggeration. You can find out more about this on various websites and social media platforms. Do not forget to visit photo exhibitions, or the nearest library. Join street photography communities. Think about whether you would like to take a course. Best of all, meet other photographers, look at their work and show them yours. It will help your development.

14

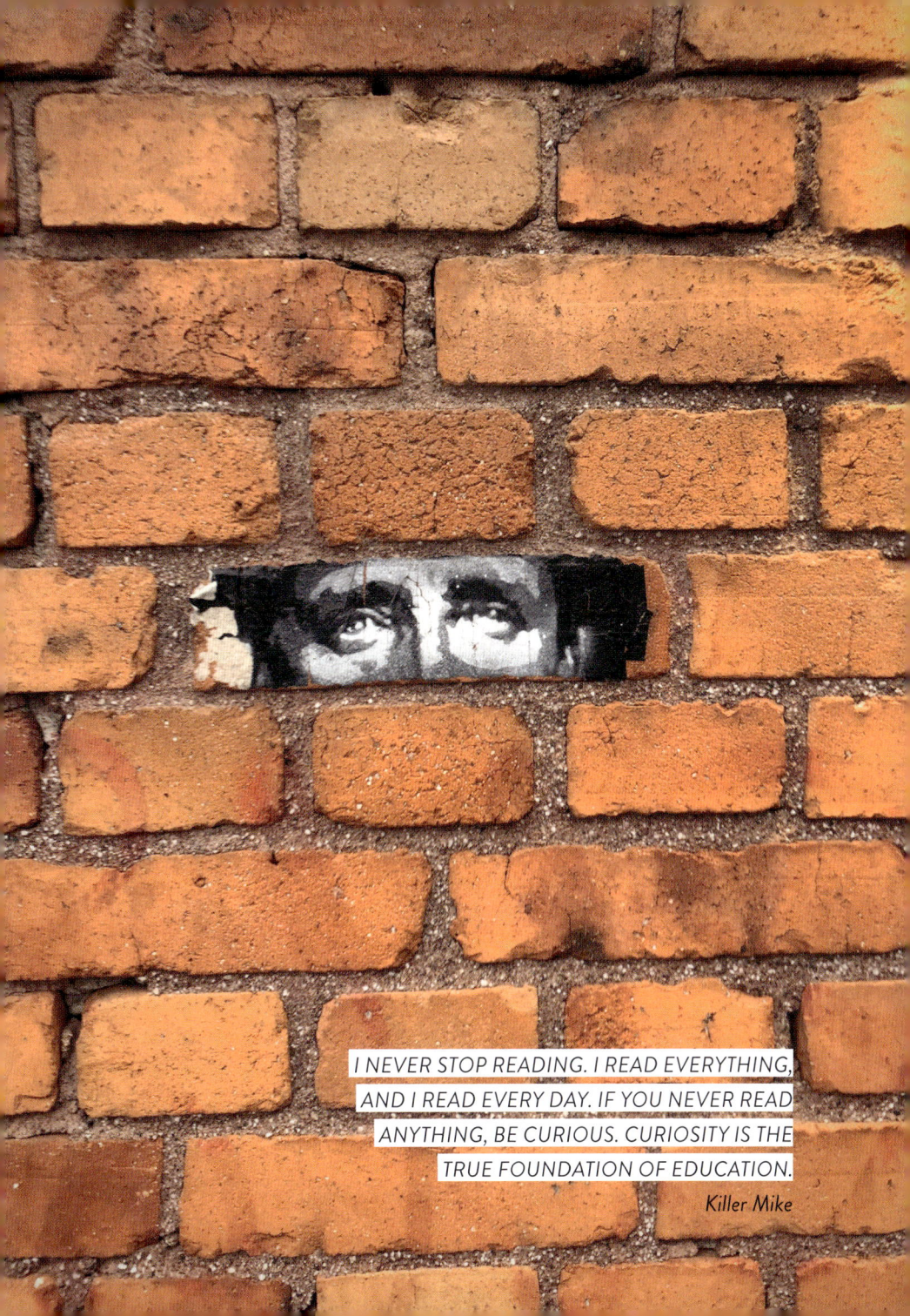

I NEVER STOP READING. I READ EVERYTHING, AND I READ EVERY DAY. IF YOU NEVER READ ANYTHING, BE CURIOUS. CURIOSITY IS THE TRUE FOUNDATION OF EDUCATION.

Killer Mike

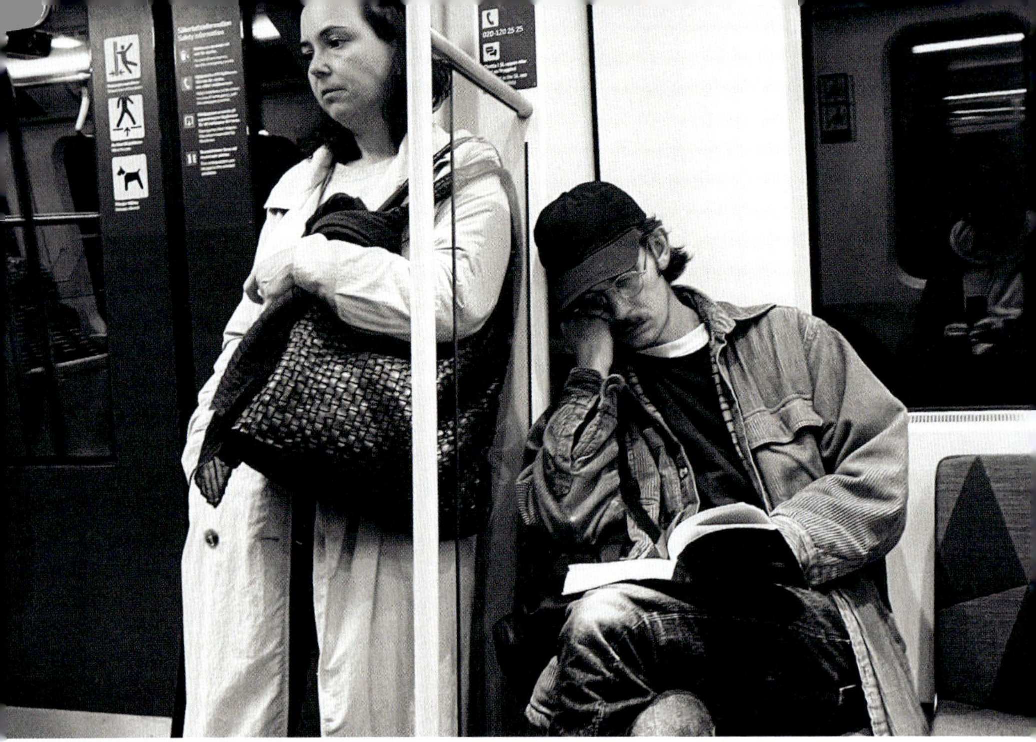
020-120 25 25

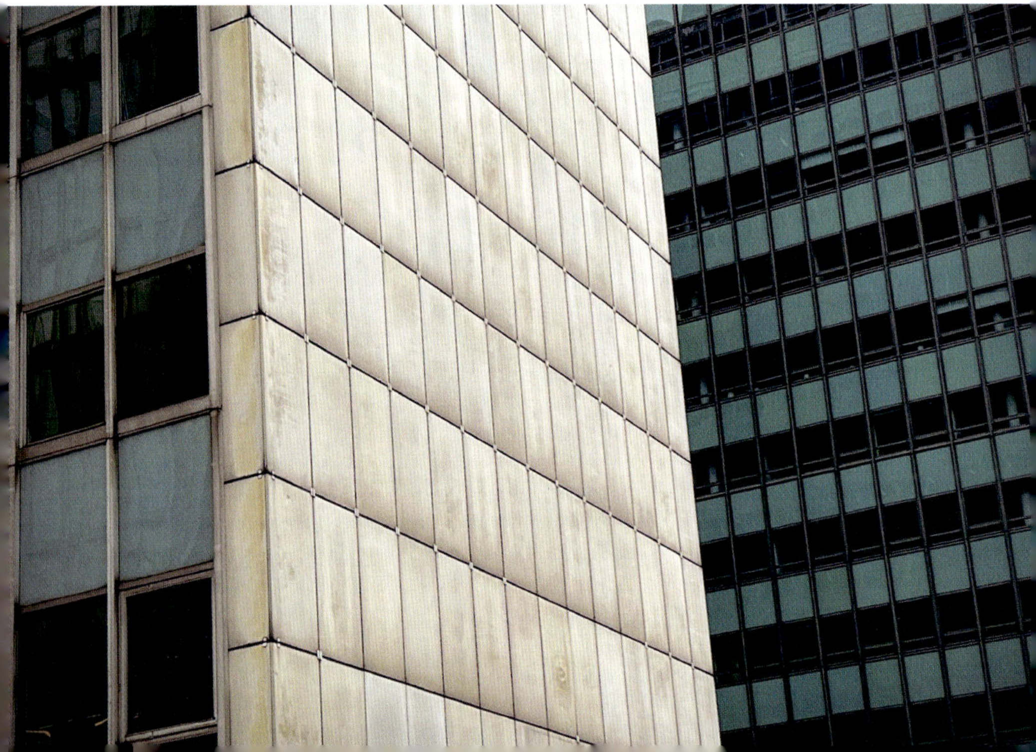

AFTER YOU HAVE STARTED

SHOW YOUR WORK. There are many ways of making your work public, *social media* is one of the most effective. If you do not yet have a social media presence, it would be a good idea to find out which platforms suit you best. Many dream of publishing a *photo book*, but it is not always easy to do unless you are well-known or able to pay for it. You need a publisher that takes care of design, marketing and distribution. You could design the book yourself or with a friend. Many different services are available. It will take longer, but you will have better control of the process – and you will definitely learn a lot along the way.

Photo books are all well and good, but they take time and are expensive. Making your own *photo fanzine* may be a simpler alternative. Or you can contact *websites* and *photo journals* that publish street photography, they are often interested in new photographers. Or you can submit your work to *competitions*. If you are lucky, your work will be on display and you will be assessed by an expert panel of judges. Find out which competition would suit you best. Do not forget to look up previous winners, and to work on your presentation.

Putting together an *exhibition* may sound over-ambitious, but it is a good idea to check out cafés, libraries, galleries and museums in your neighbourhood. Ask what they normally show. If you're lucky, they may have an opportunity or some free space. Or exhibit at home or at a friend's house. Is it possible to project you work on a wall outdoors? Print posters? Before you begin to pitch your work, it is a good idea to spend some time describing what makes *your* images interesting. Give them punchy, thought-provoking titles. Describe how you work, your target audience and why you want to show your pictures now. Practice your "elevator pitch".

KEEP TRACK OF YOUR WORK. This goes without saying, but I'm one of many who have been careless. After a while it is hard to find what you are looking for, and worse case scenario, pictures go missing. Cameras are lost or stolen, memory cards stop working and mobiles break.

To avoid this:

1. *Backup your work!* One easy way is to automatically upload it to a cloud service. Or you can use external hard disks. To keep your work perfectly safe, save it on three different units and keep two of them in separate places.

2. *Organise your archive.* The pictures need to be searchable, so tag them as soon as possible after the picture is taken. Date and location are a must, this can be done more or less automatically. Regardless of the method and media you choose, the information needs to include: *What* (information about what the picture shows, people's names, buildings, etc.). *How* (any aspects that are important to publication, such as restrictions or conditions). Label your pictures using a project name or theme.

18

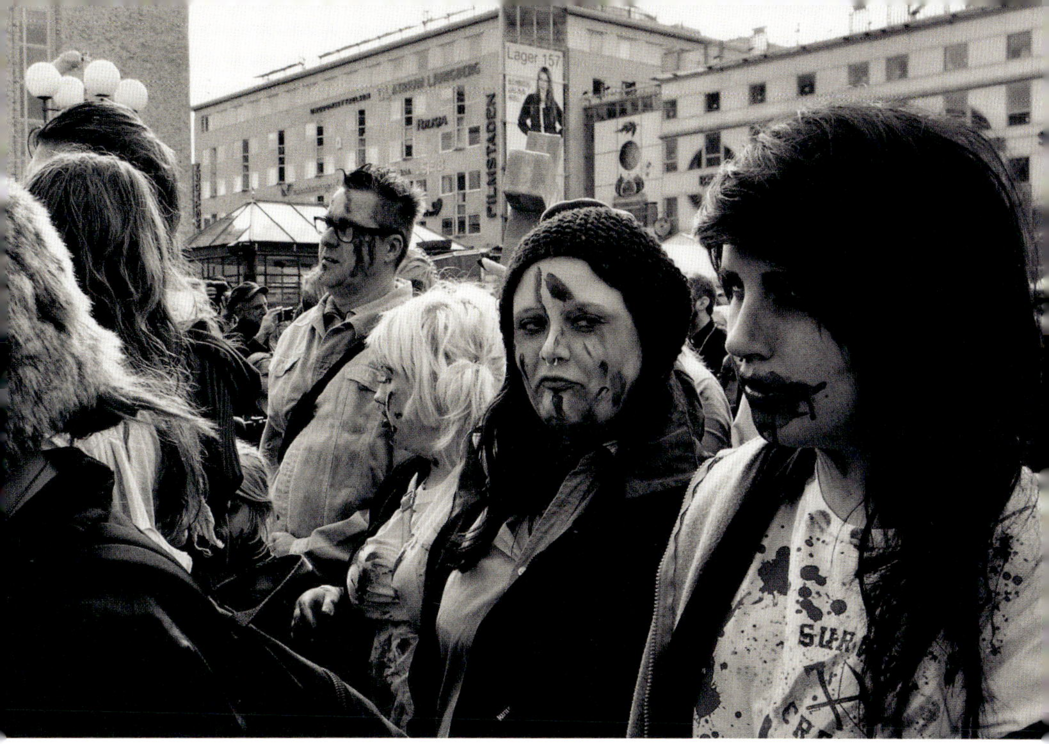
Lager 157
FILMSTADEN

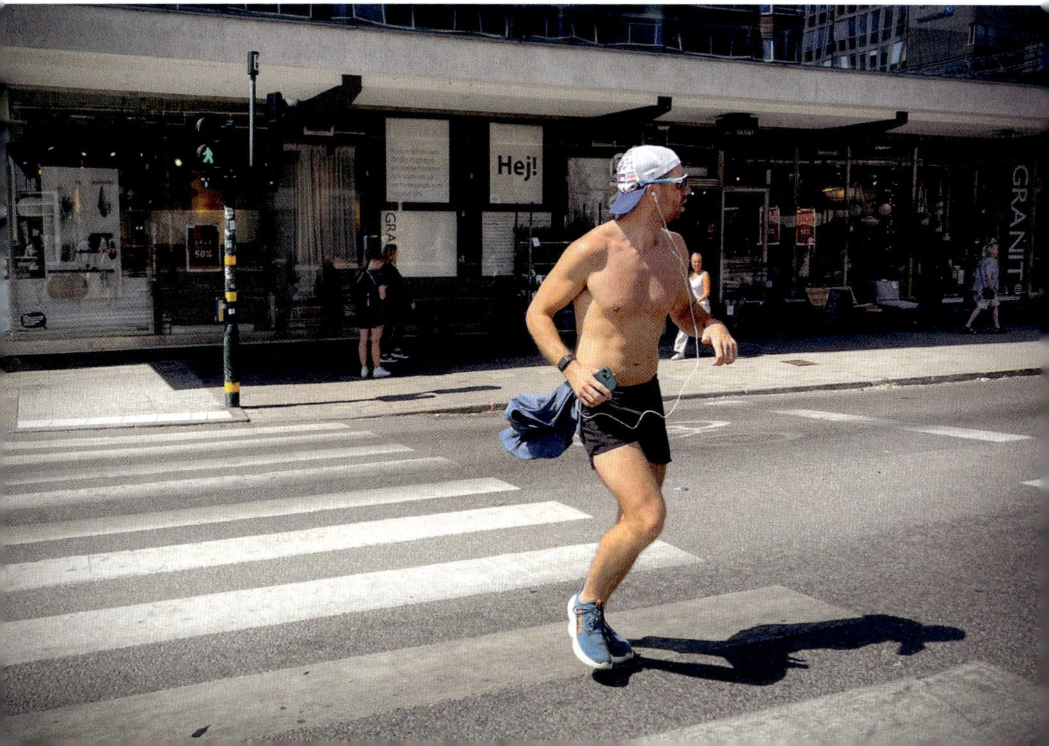
Hej!
GRANIT
50%

50 CRE
CHALL
THAT...

EATIVE
ENGES

will make you a better street photographer!

Each exercise invites you to explore perspectives and experiment with content, style, lighting and composition. It is not only about shooting pictures, it is about getting out there and discovering stories in the city. Do one exercise a day, a week, or when you are stuck and in need of inspiration.

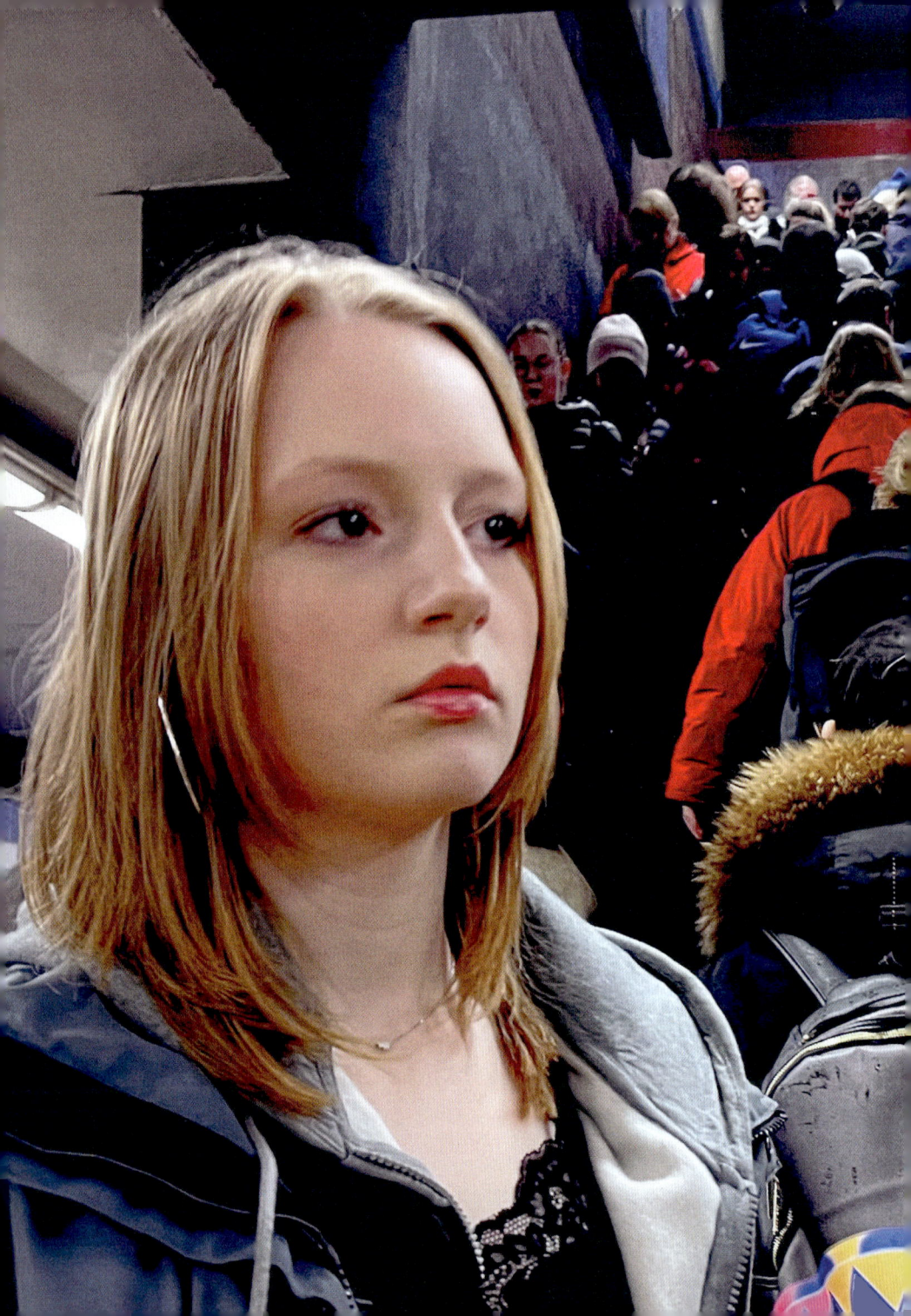

1. BLEND INTO THE CROWD

CROWDED PLACES offer great variation in terms of motifs. You will encounter more movement and life. It is easier not to be noticed, if that is what you want. Events, concerts and demonstrations, or train stations, markets, and amusement parks, can be fun to test. The history of street photography is full of stories from this kind of places. The work of Robert Doisneau, Garry Winogrand and Diane Arbus are only a few examples.

VISIT A CROWDED AREA

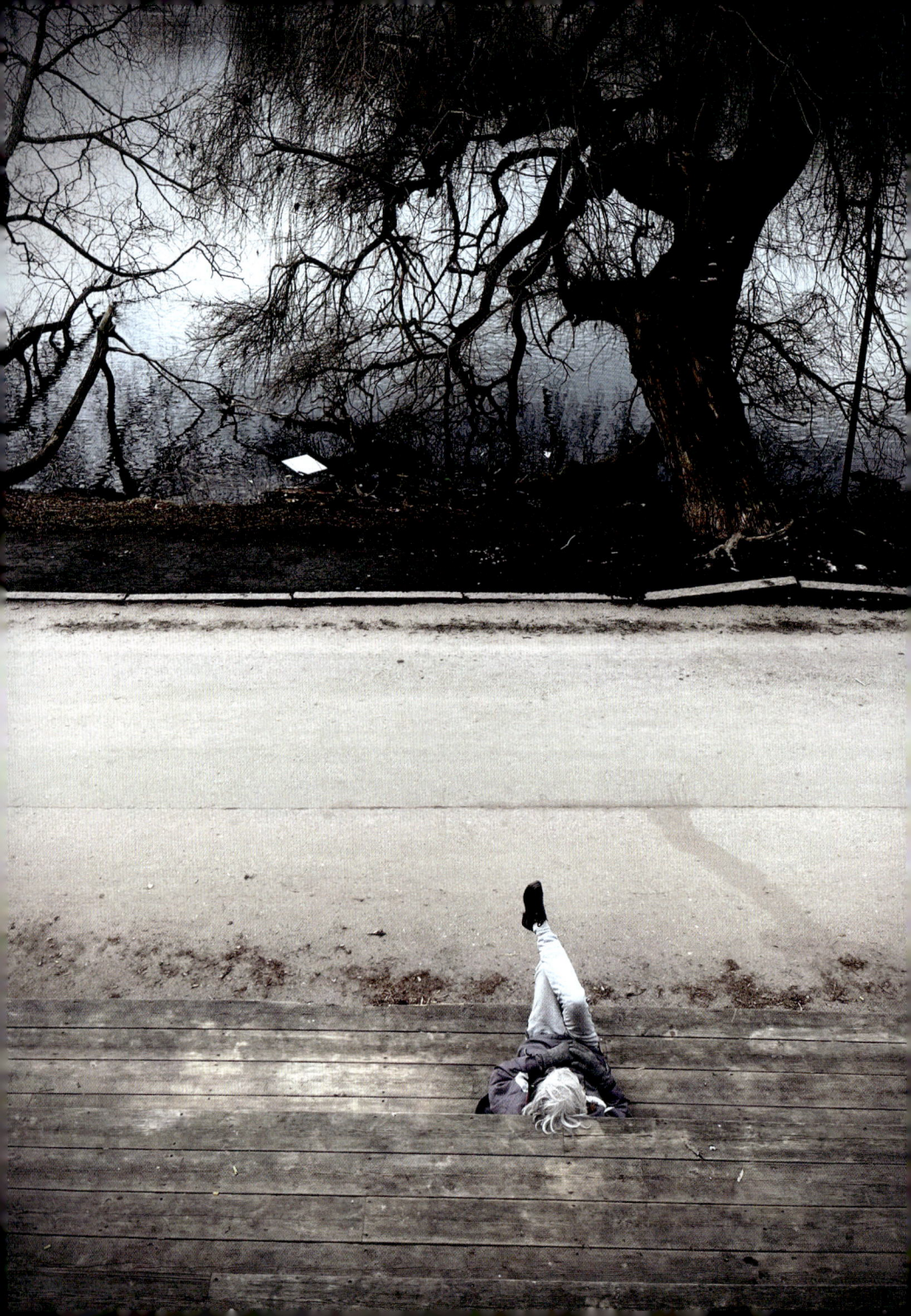

2. CHANGE YOUR PERSPECTIVE

GET USED TO seeing things from a different perspective. You can reduce something and enhance something else just by moving the camera a little to the left or right. It is basically about not always shooting from the same position, usually face-height (normal perspective), and instead moving closer or further away from the subject. You can lower the camera (worm's eye view) or raise it (bird's eye view). More on perspective on page 32.

More on perspective on page 32.

CAPTURE A MOTIF FROM THREE
DIFFERENT PERSPECTIVES

3. WRITE A MANIFEST

NOW THAT STREET photography is more popular than ever, it may be a good idea to think about your own role and write a manifest about what you want to achieve. Make big plans, but it does not have to be long. Why do you like photographing in the street? What do you want to communicate with your pictures? Any principles that are particularly important to you? Write it down.

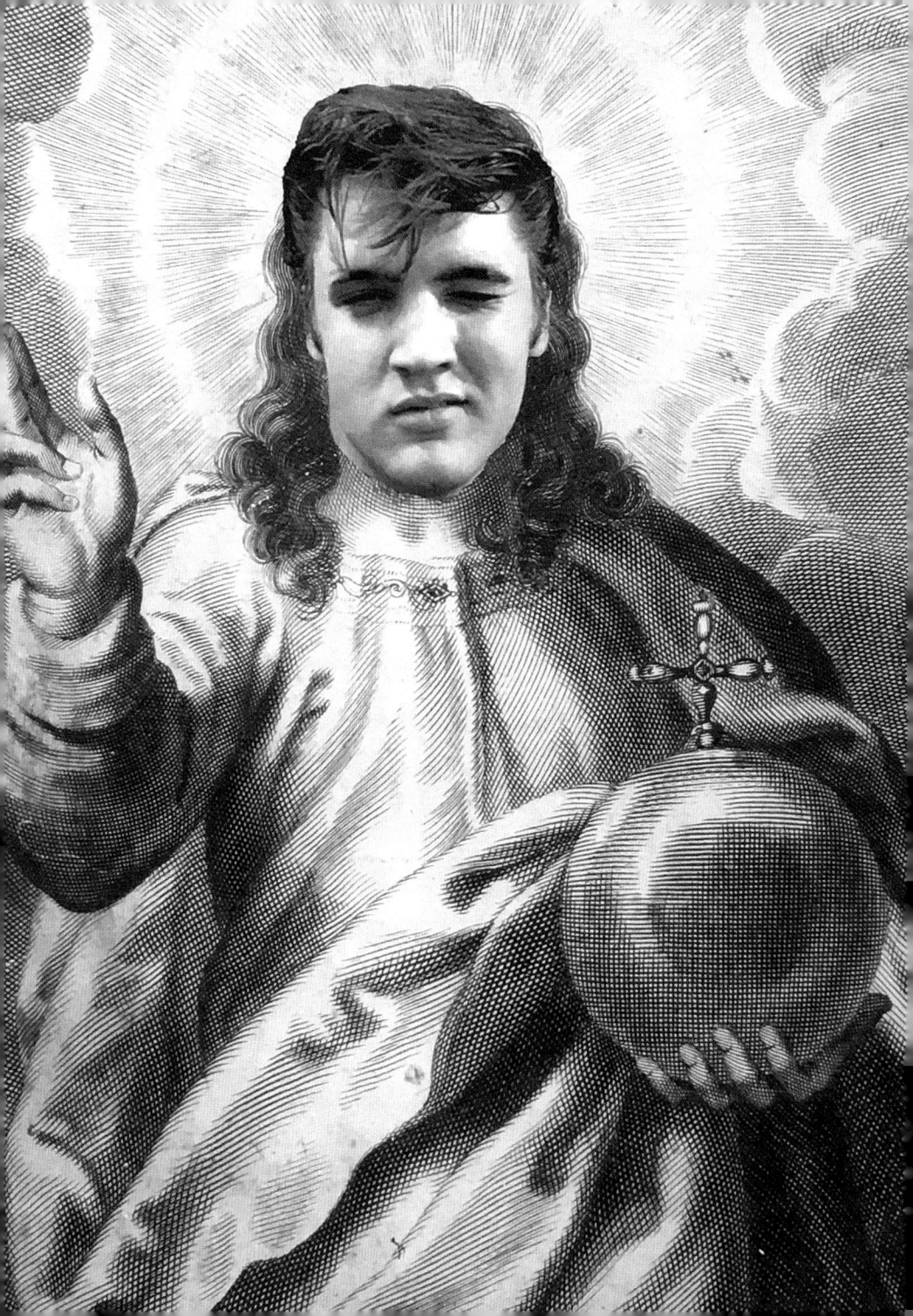

4. THINK THEMATICALLY

A THEME CAN serve as a through-line, supporting you in knowing what not to photograph. It is not always easy to think of a theme, sometimes it finds you. General themes include travelling, architecture, consumption, or fitness. You can use emotions such as anticipation, happiness, anxiety, or love. Or you can see the city as an evolving drama, a zoo, a hideout or a place for contemplation, encounters, or crime. A simpler version: describe a colour, shape, or structure – wall tiles, for example. A theme makes it easier to edit and select images for a portfolio, an exhibition, or a picture story. My own interest in street photography has given me direction and inspiration for new ideas and projects.

MY THEME IS _____

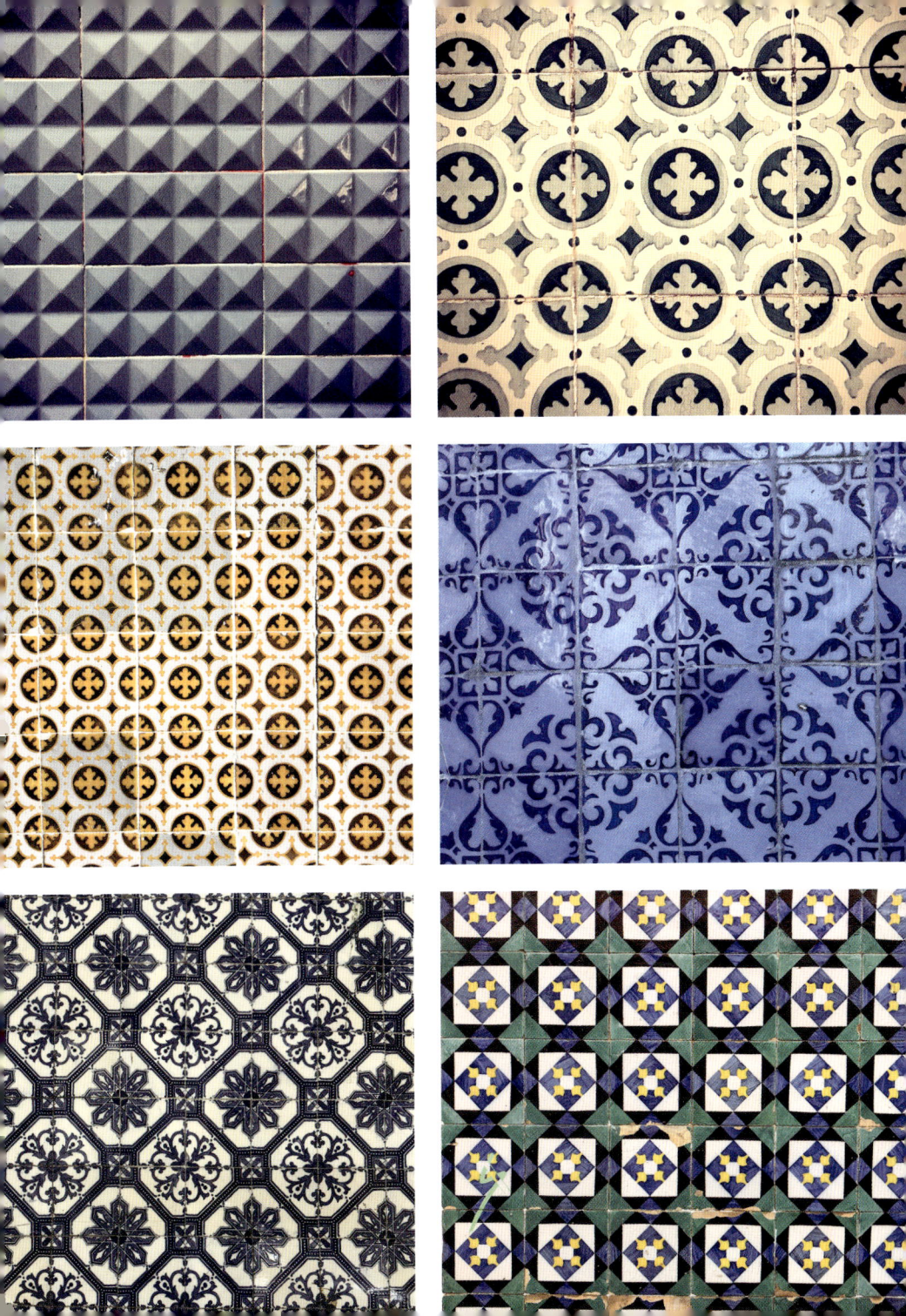

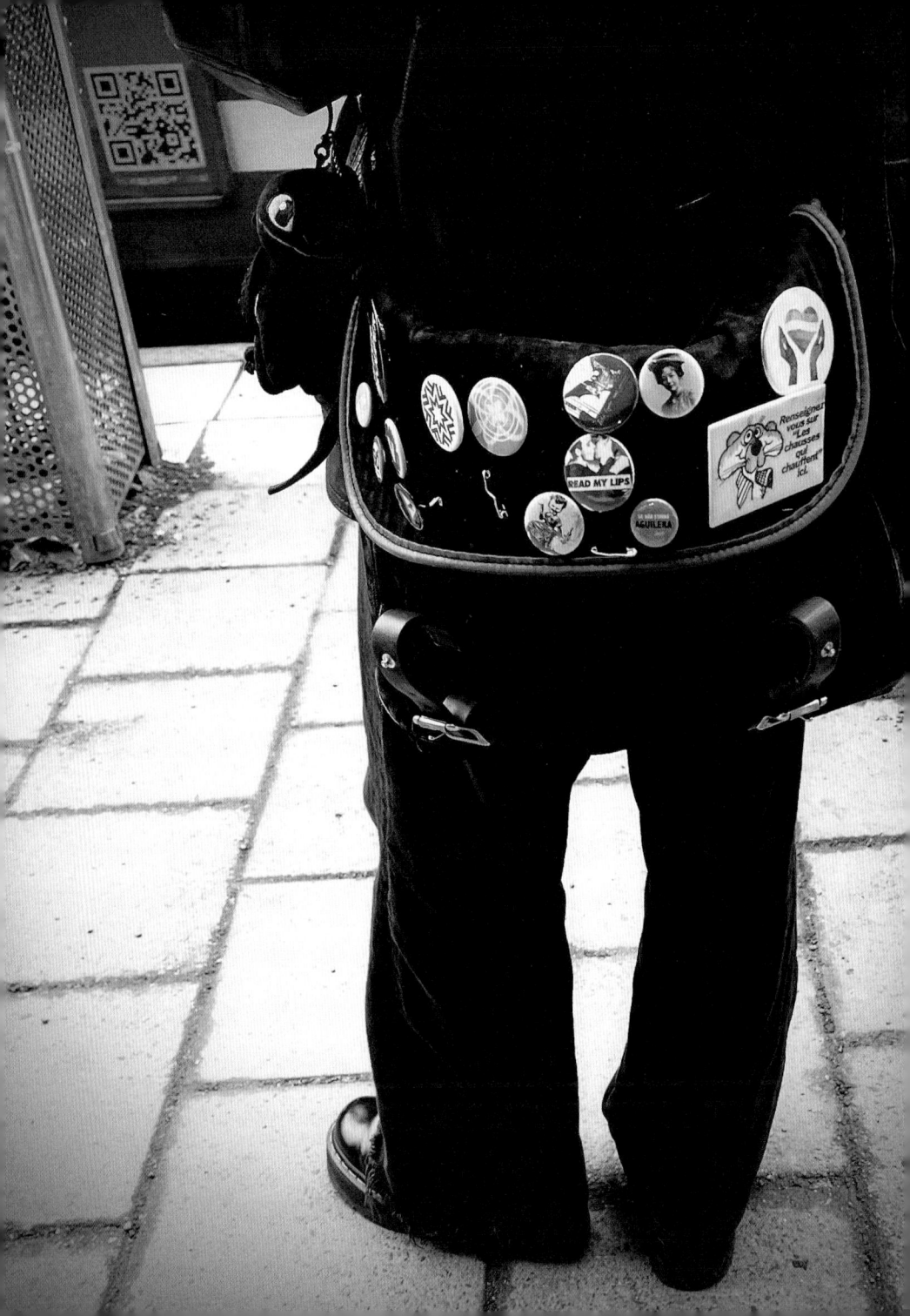

5. ZOOM IN

THERE IS MORE to discover than you might think in the minutia of street life. It is easy to miss things if you visit the same place often. If you train yourself in the art of noticing details, you will break the routine and discover a richer visual world, the city's microcosm. A seemingly unimportant matter becomes something bigger. A small detail has a story of its own. You can often find your motifs by being more attentive to what appears in your peripheral vision, where you do not normally look. Zoom in. Zoom in more.

ANYBODY CAN BE A GREAT PHOTOGRAPHER IF THEY ZOOM IN ENOUGH ON WHAT THEY LOVE.
David Bailey

6. ZOOM OUT

TAKE A FEW STEPS back, and you will open up a wider perspective by moving your attention from the details to the whole. There are many ways to zoom out: change to a wide angle lens or walk further back. This allows you to tell a more detailed story about context and atmosphere. You can also take pictures that include more elements, for example in the foreground or background.

*BEST WIDE ANGLE LENS?
TWO STEPS BACKWARD.
LOOK FOR THE 'AH HA'.*
Ernst Haas

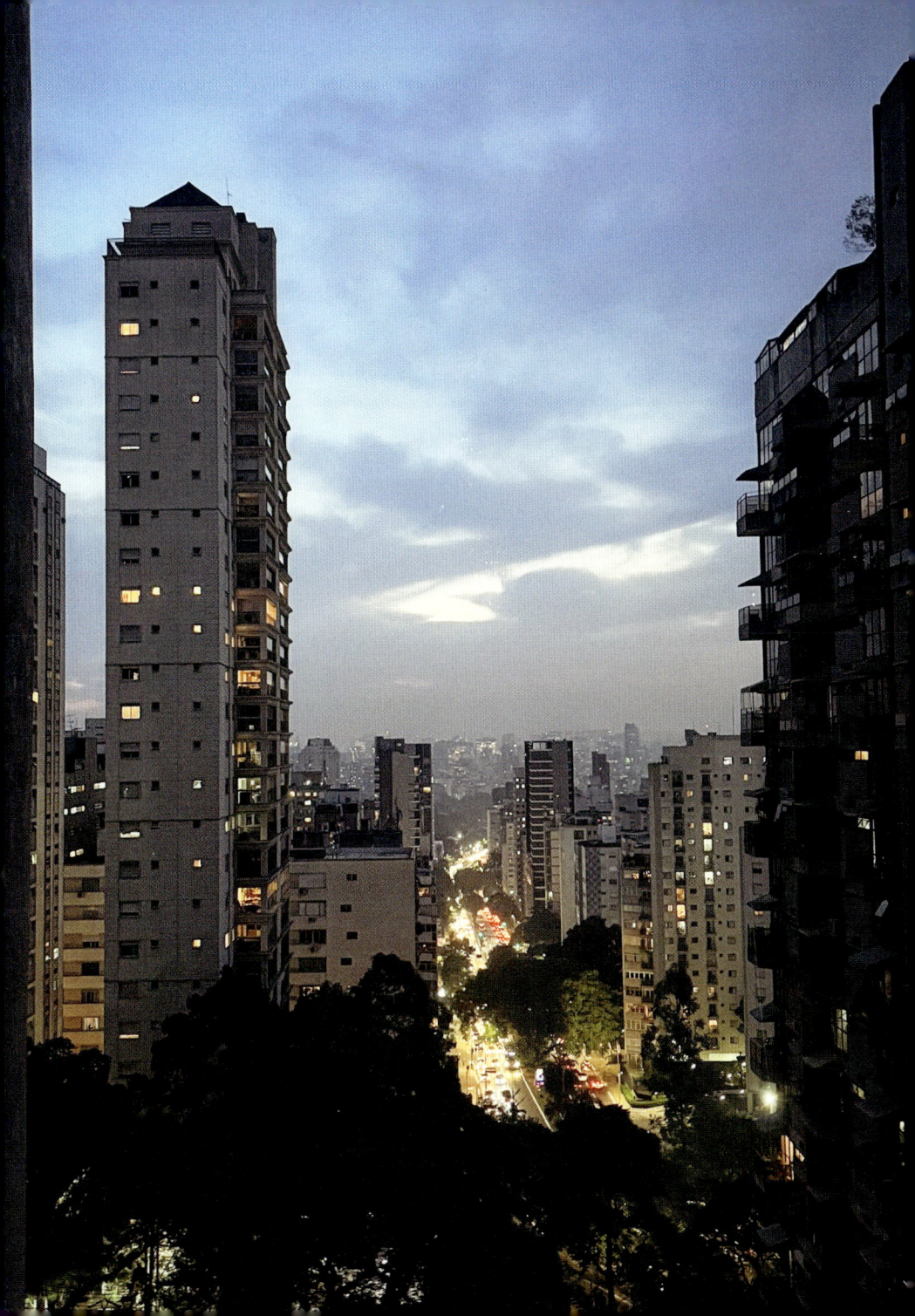

7. STAND STILL

STREET PHOTOGRAPHERS move around a lot. But there is good reason to stop and let the motifs come to you. So, do not run about, wait for the right moment, which can be hard if you are impatient. You will discover new things. Stop somewhere you had not planned to stop, or where the background adds to the general impression.

SOMETIMES I FEEL LIKE THE WORLD IS A PLACE I BOUGHT A TICKET TO. IT IS A BIG SHOW FOR ME AS IF IT WOULDN'T HAPPEN IF I WAS NOT THERE WITH A CAMERA.

Garry Winogrand

STAND STILL FOR 30 MINUTES

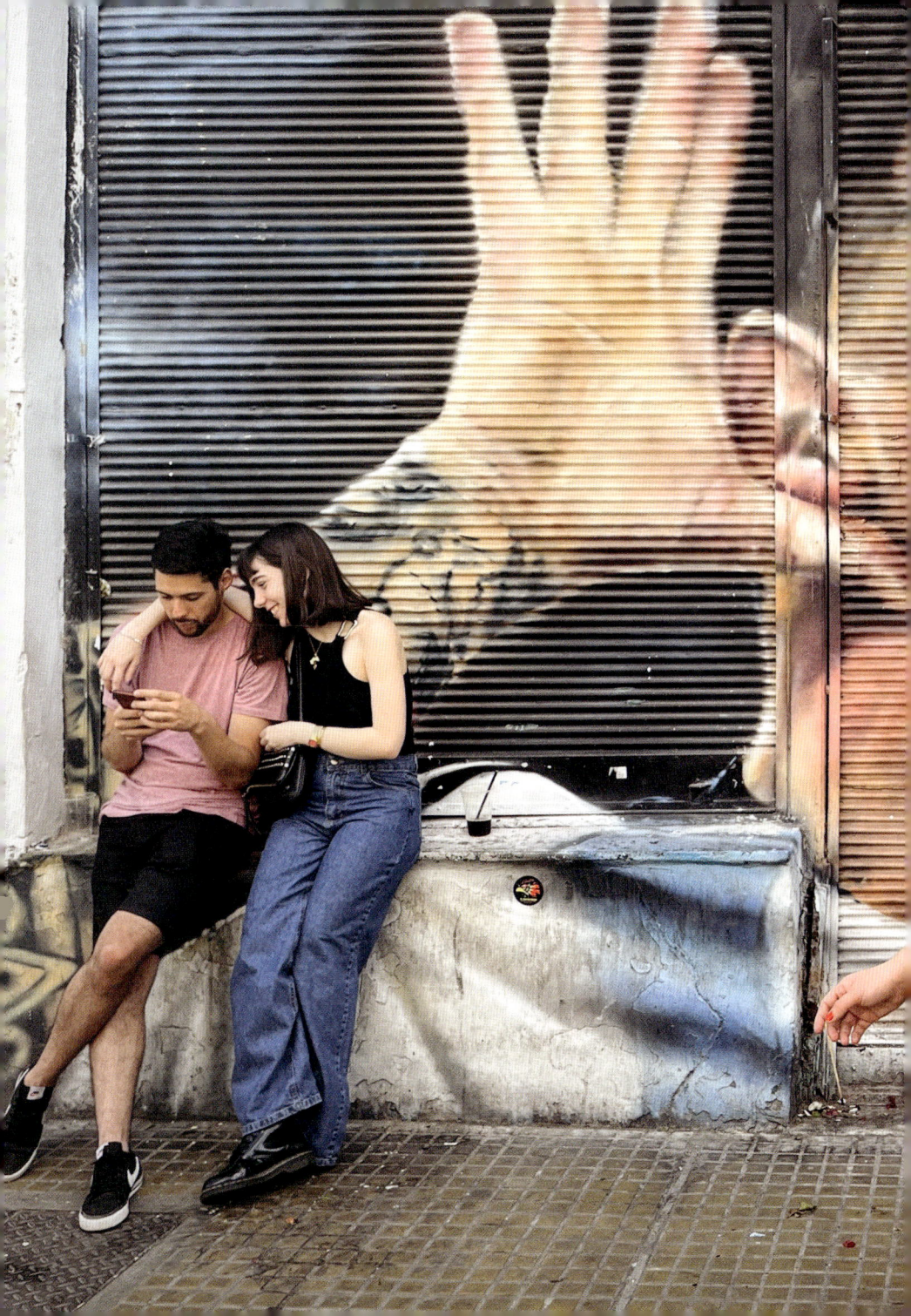

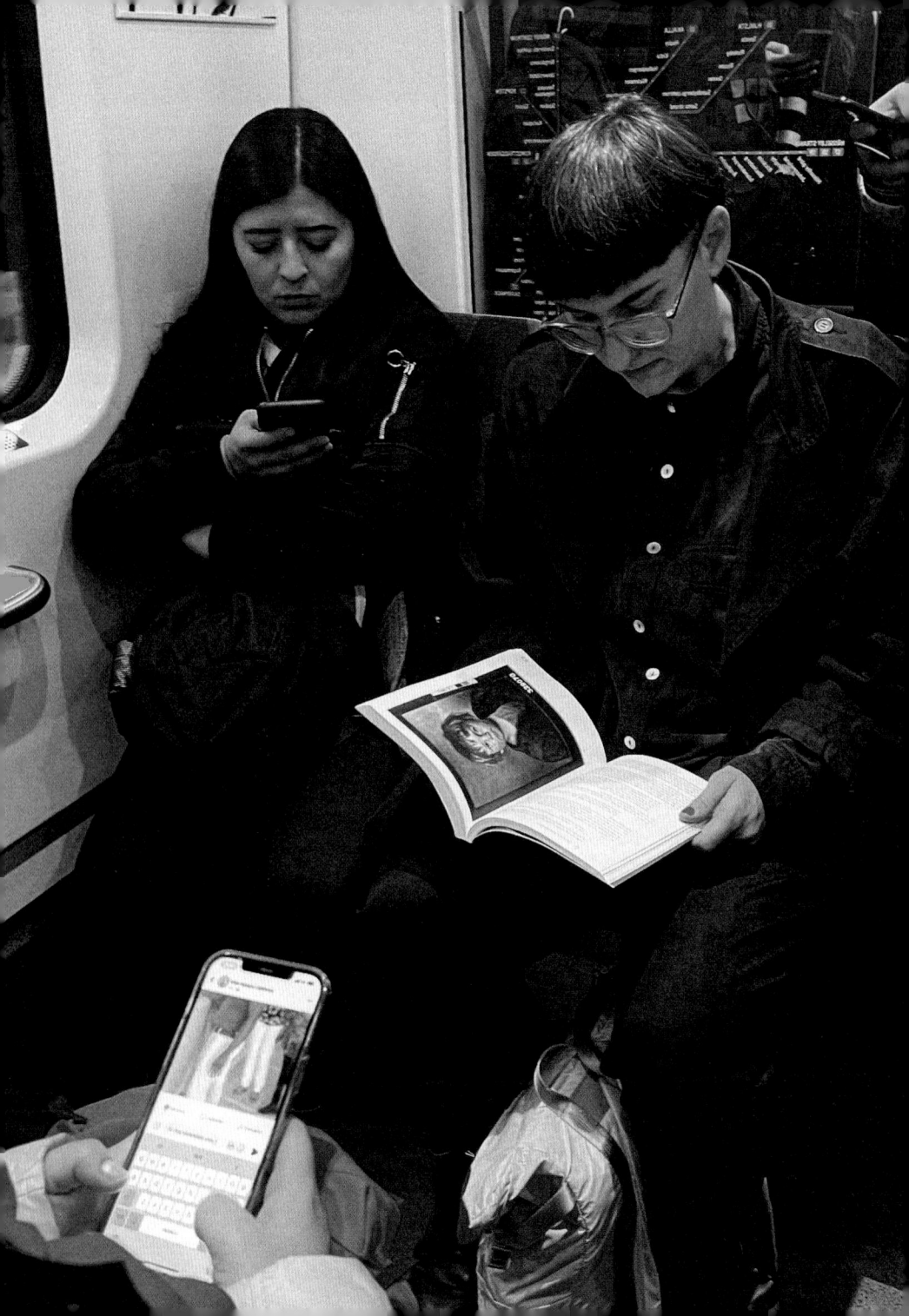

8. LOOK FOR CONTRASTS

OPPOSITES HELP OUR brains to interpret images. By distinguishing between elements, the brain creates structure and meaning. Photographs often contain a lot of conflicting information. It may appear in terms of content, when we look at the differences between wealth and poverty, hope and anxiety, love and hate. It can also be between light and dark, focus and blur. Focusing on contrasting realities is an effective tool when you want people to notice your image and in communicating emotions and a particular message.

9. CAPTURE THE SPIRIT OF THE TIME

ONE OF THE MORE fascinating aspects of street photography is that it automatically captures the transitory spirit of the time. Perhaps that is why older street photography is so popular. Nostalgia, reflection, and information offer clues to our own background and that of the city. Even "simple" images become more interesting with age. It is of course not always easy to distinguish the characteristics of your time, but you can train your vision by thinking in terms of categories: fashion, advertising, or technology, or look for a place that is undergoing change.

FIND AN EXAMPLE OF SOMETHING TYPICAL OF YOUR TIME

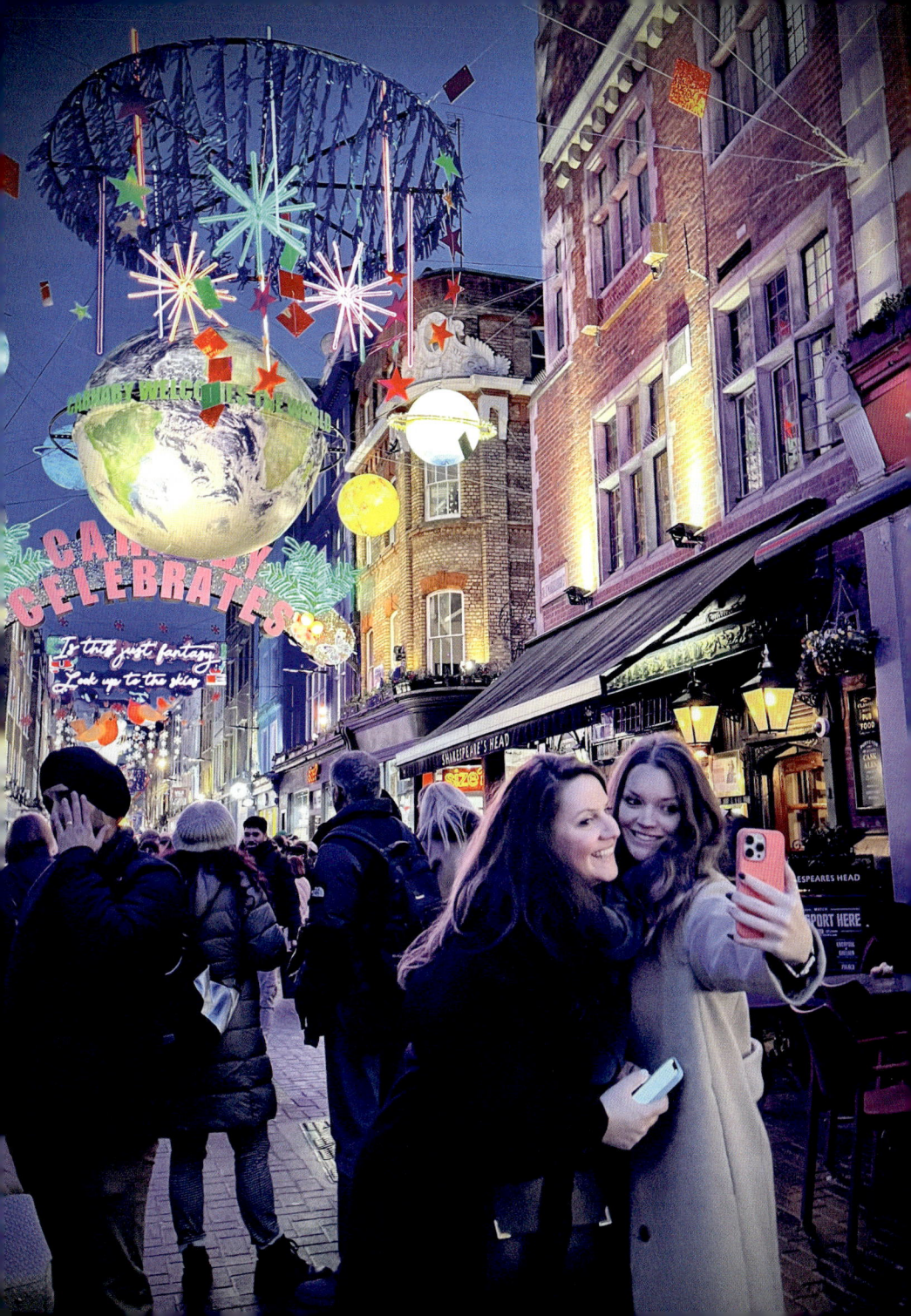

10. LOOK FOR LEADING LINES

MUCH HAS BEEN said about the importance of lines to image composition and how it relates to the way we experience it. Some believe lines help us interpret an image as they generate movement and order. According to others this rationale is too theoretical: it is better to go with feeling and intuition than to put too much emphasis on composition. Both points-of-view are valid, but if you search for lines, you will soon realise how much they affect the outcome. Start by exploring some of the most common ones: horizontal, vertical, diagonal and curved.

BASE YOUR IMAGE ON
DOMINANT LINES IN THE CITY

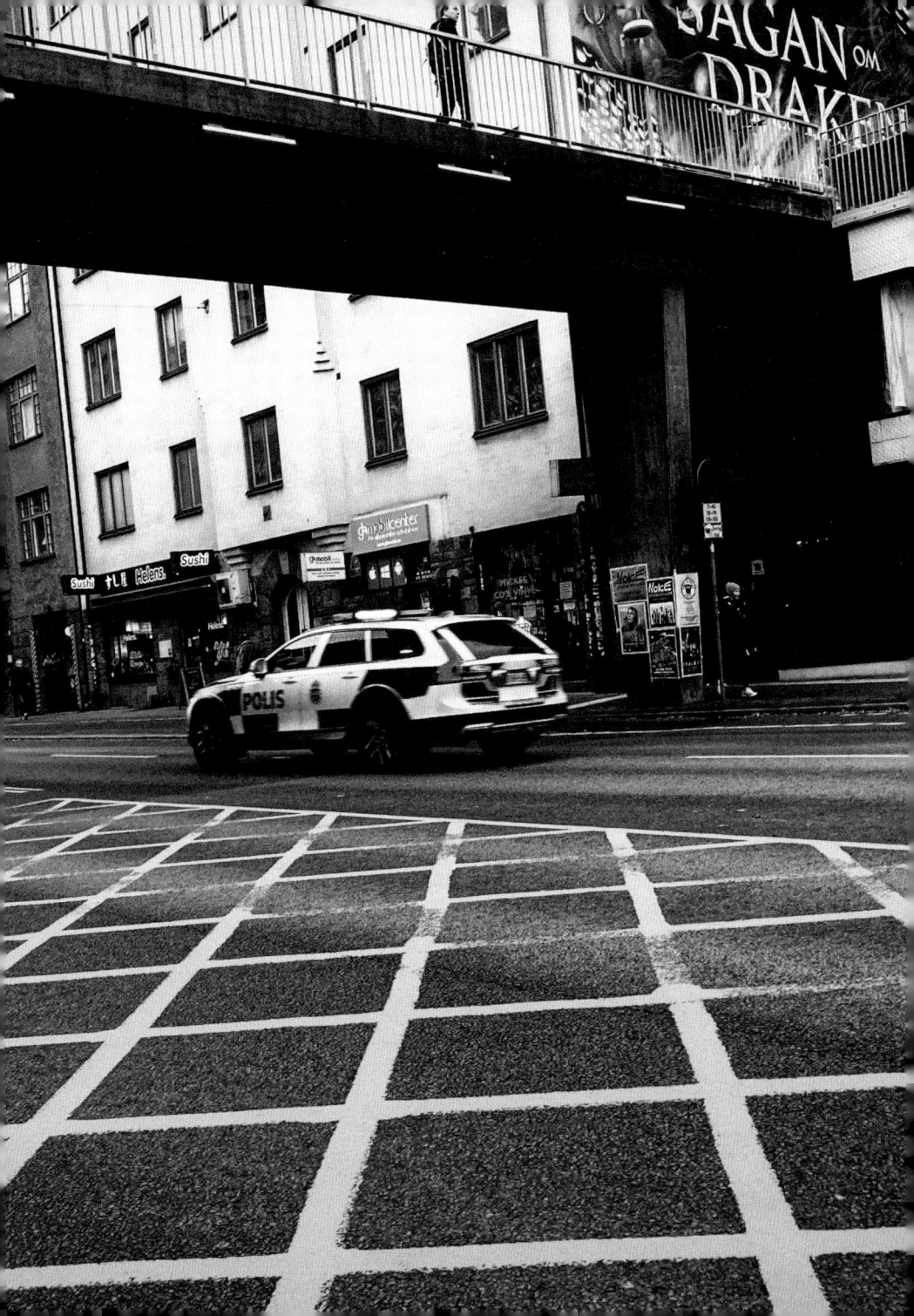

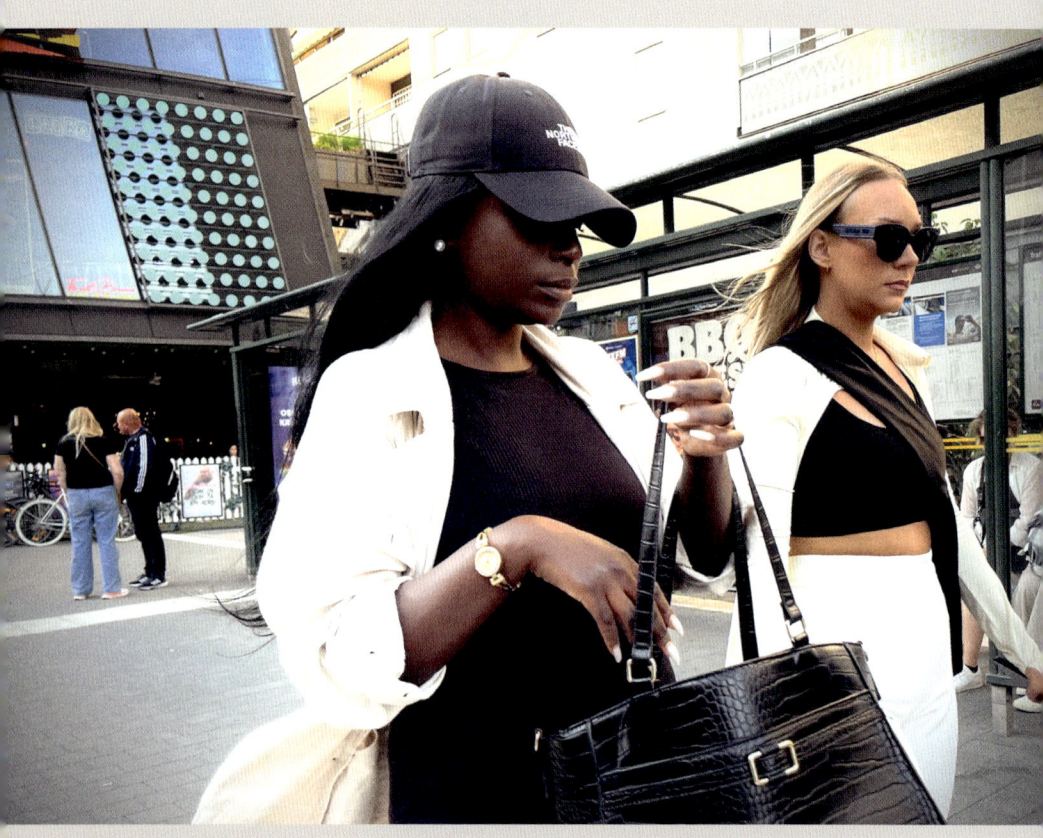

11. CHANGE YOUR SPECIALTY

IF YOUR ATTITUDE to "real" street photograph is not too dogmatic, you should test different styles. It is fun and you learn something by changing your specialty or walking in someone else's shoes. If you are a documentary photographer one day, you can be a fashion photographer the next. If you are a portrait photographer today you can be a nature photographer tomorrow, or maybe a sports photographer next week. And so on. Maybe you take the opportunity to explore a subgenre, such as portrait or urban exploration.

TODAY I AM A _____ PHOTOGRAPHER

12. TRY JUXTAPOSITION

JUXTAPOSITION IS A fancy word for playing with two or several elements. Many street photographers use this to tell a story that can be interpreted by, for example, portraying old and new or happiness and grief in the same image. Juxtaposition is a common term for showing humorous or strange events that occur in the street. Combining two elements that are very similar, or that do not quite go together can communicate a sense of irony or surprise. See also *Look for Contrasts* on page 37.

TAKE A PICTURE USING JUXTAPOSITION

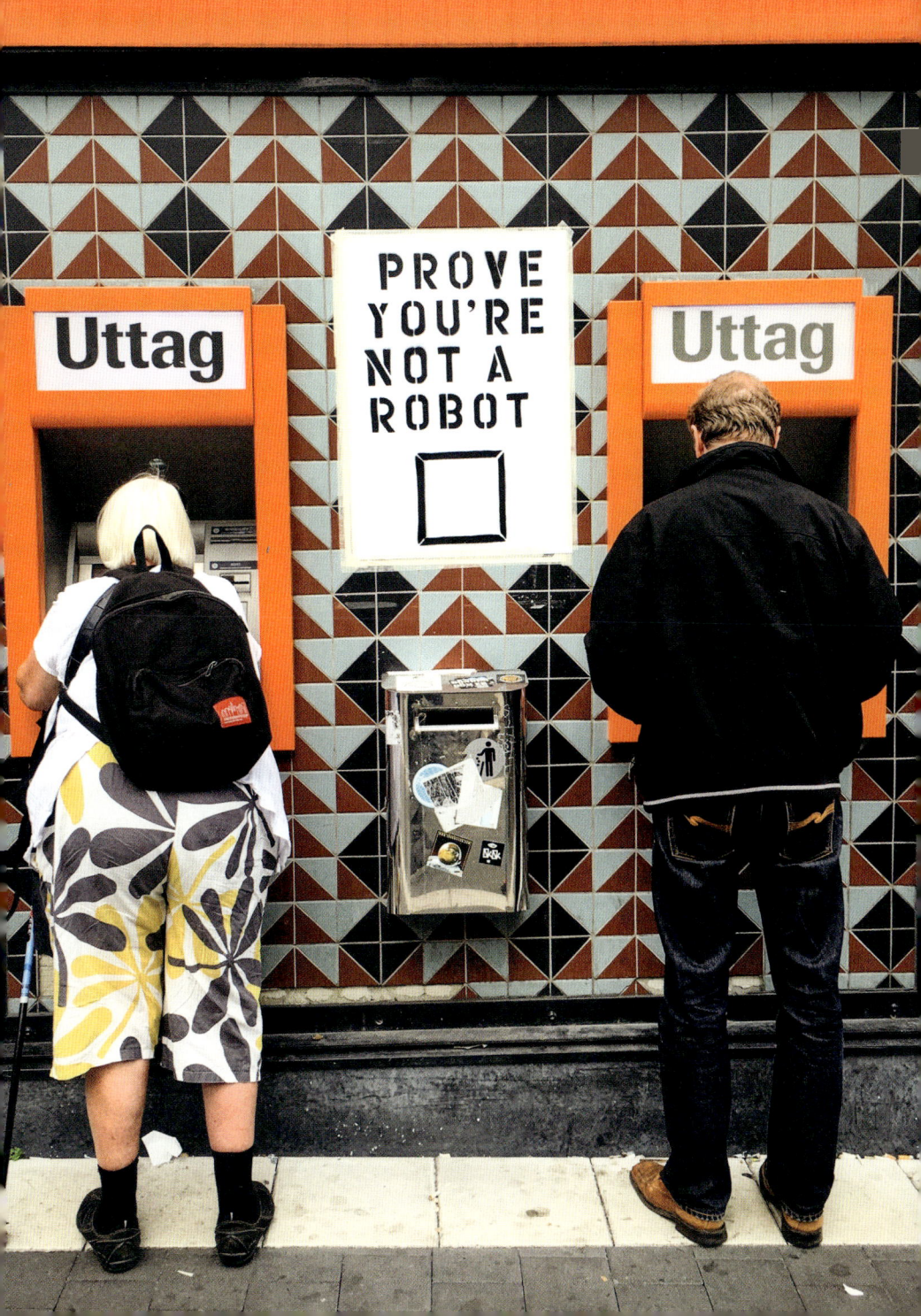

13. COMPOSE IN THE CAMERA

TO BETTER UNDERSTAND image composition, try to compose your picture when you take it. In this case you do not shoot from the hip, use the view finder instead. Out in the street you become a little less anonymous, but you gain control of your composition. This is a simple exercise. The image is ready as soon as you have captured it. Cropping it as you shoot makes you more focused and present. Here are some tips for achieving variation:

- Accentuate the motif
- Try different perspectives
- Keep the background clean
- Look for lines and structures – What creates balance or imbalance?
- What about movement – Should you accentuate it or tone it down?
- Create depth – What is in the foreground, middle-distance and background?

I NEVER SHOOT WITHOUT USING THE VIEWFINDER.
Garry Winogrand

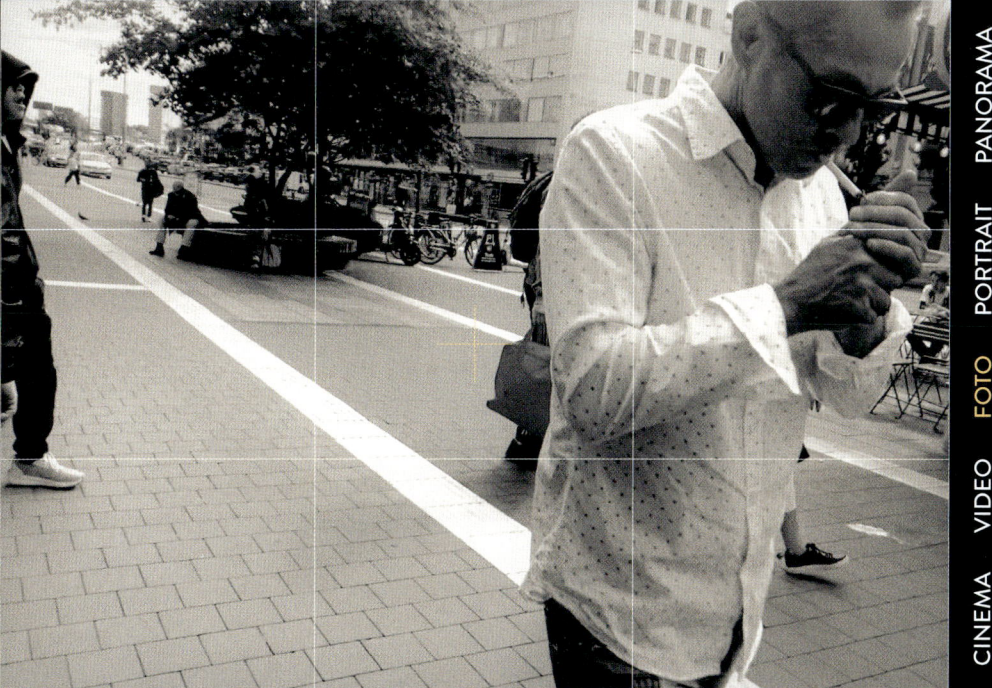

14. BREAK THE RULES

ANYONE SETTING OUT as a street photographer, or any other kind of photographer, will soon discover that there is a profusion of ideas about what can be considered a good photograph. It may have to do with composition, lens, style or motif. You should listen to others, learn the theory and how to use your equipment. But if you follow the advice of others too closely, your pictures may become too predictable. You risk losing your playfulness. It is not always necessary to:

- Use the golden mean
- Have good light
- Have focus
- Have a clean background
- Avoid backlighting
- Give room for movement
- Hold the camera straight
- Centralise the motif
- Have the correct exposure
- Have a straight horizon

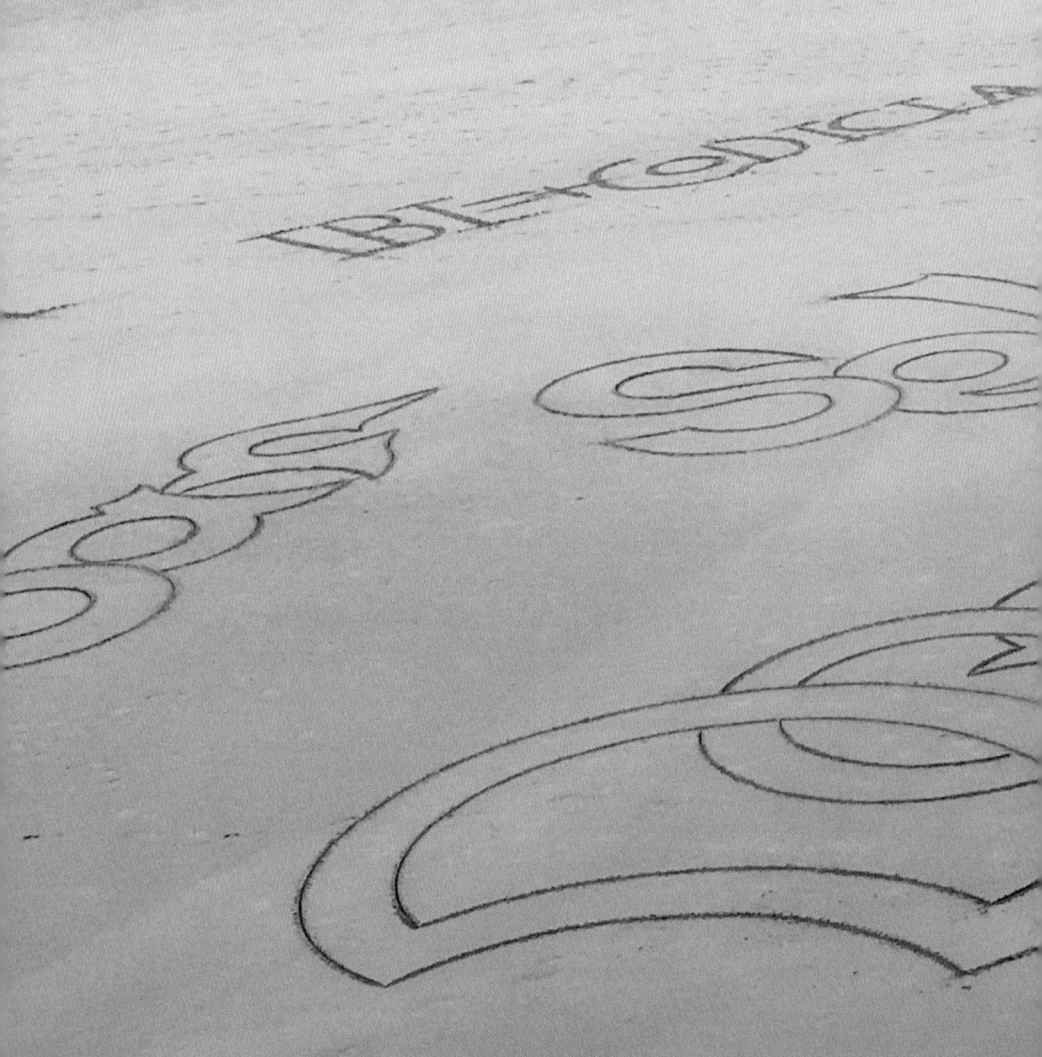

50   **CREATE A PICTURE WITH FEW DETAILS**

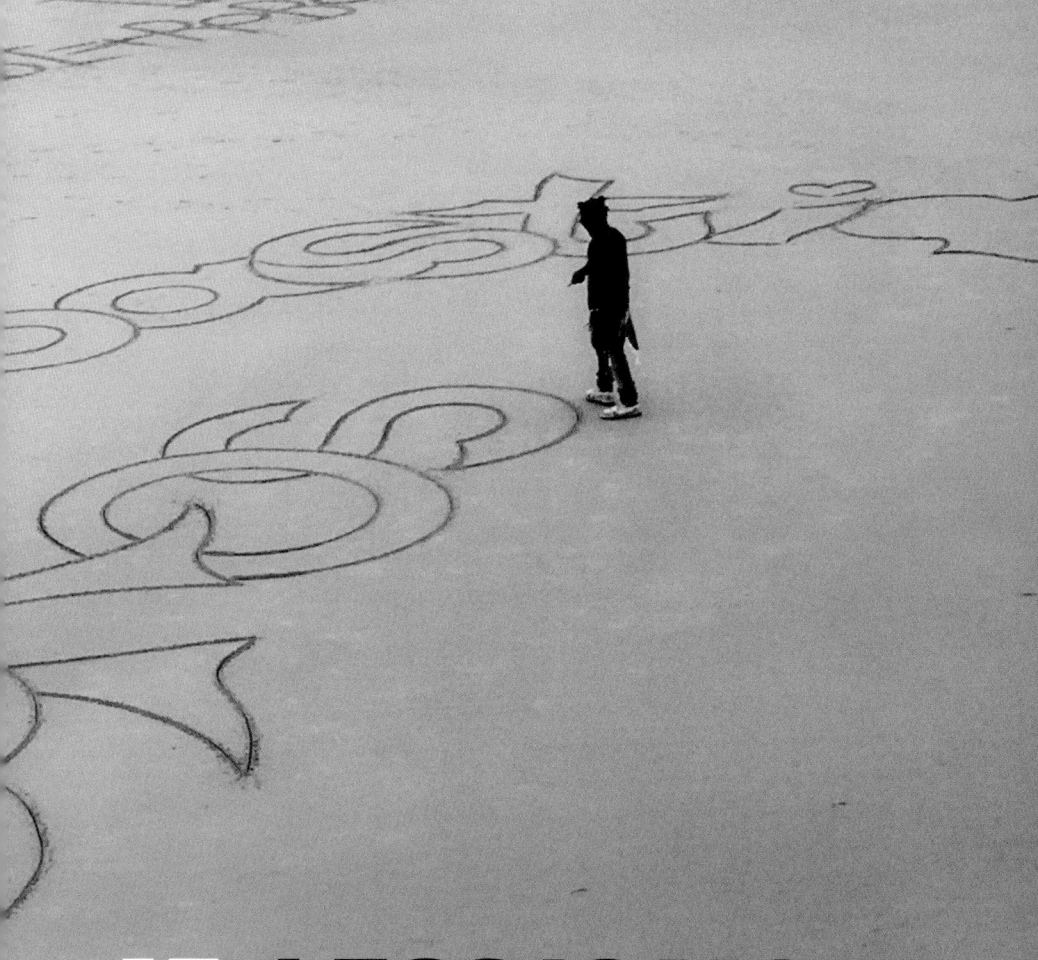

15. LESS IS MORE

SOME LIKE TO fill their pictures with content and details, others like to keep them simple and without distractions. A minimalistic street photographer looks for clean compositions without visual noise. The purpose is to avoid unnecessary detail and allow the observer to focus on a core element. Should you want to create this kind of image, you can work with clean backgrounds, a limited colour palette and negative space (areas of free space that isolate the motif and add balance and harmony). Fan Ho was a pioneer within this genre.

16. MORE OF EVERYTHING

IF YOU GET tired of minimalism you can look for the opposite in maximalist photography. Stop caring about simplicity and sparseness and fill your pictures with content. You "visually cram" it with a lot of detail, figures, colours and textures for a sense of over-abundance, richness and complexity. The way you sometimes experience the city. Be inspired by Alexander Webb's imagery, which is full of people, movement, and colour.

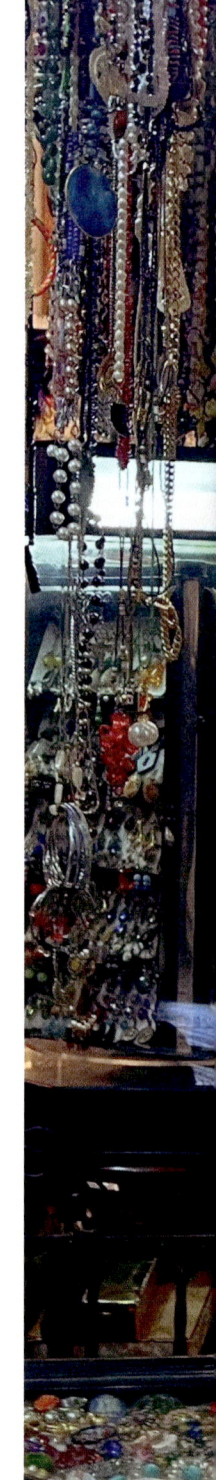

THE MOST ABUNDANT PICTURE WINS!

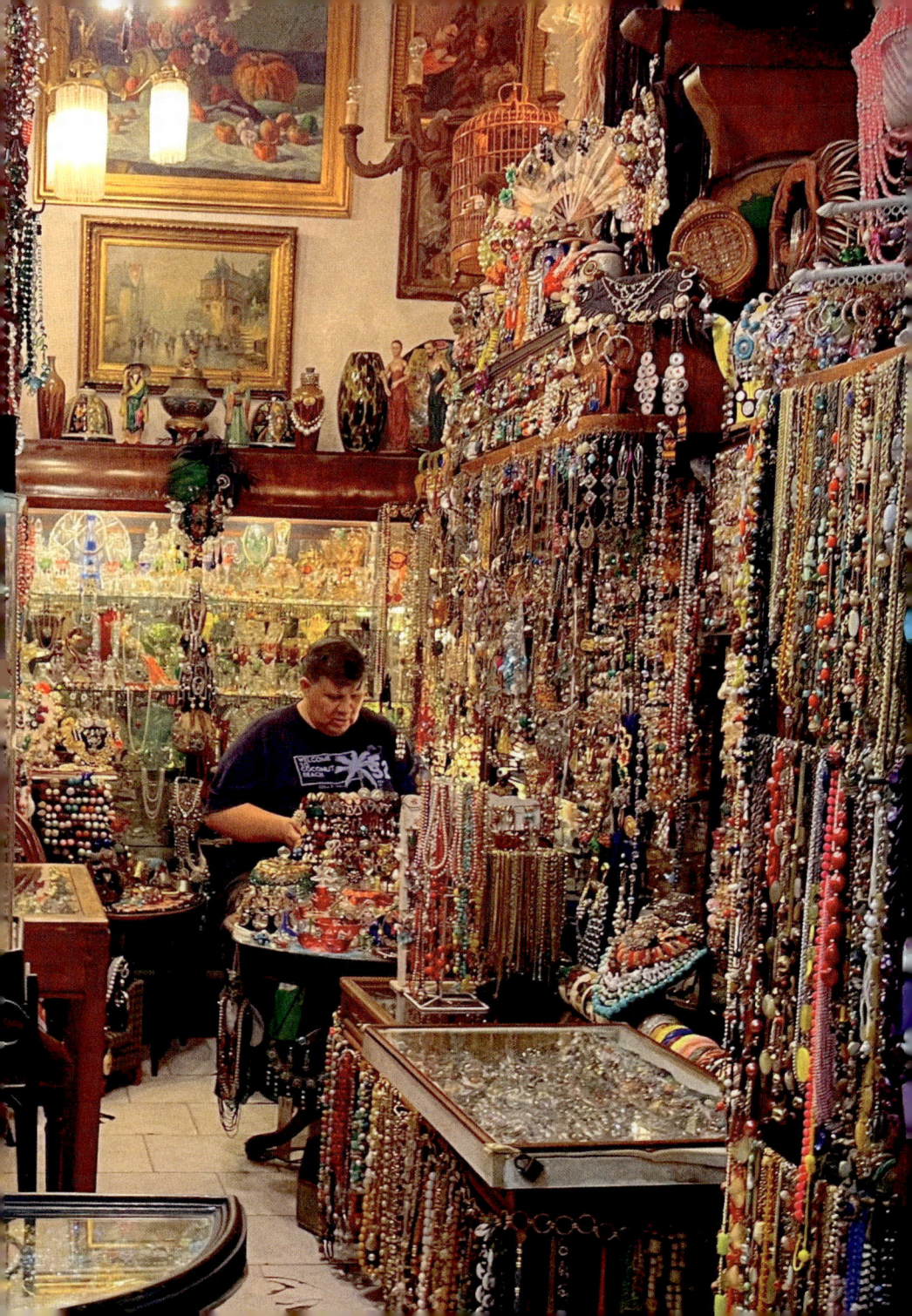

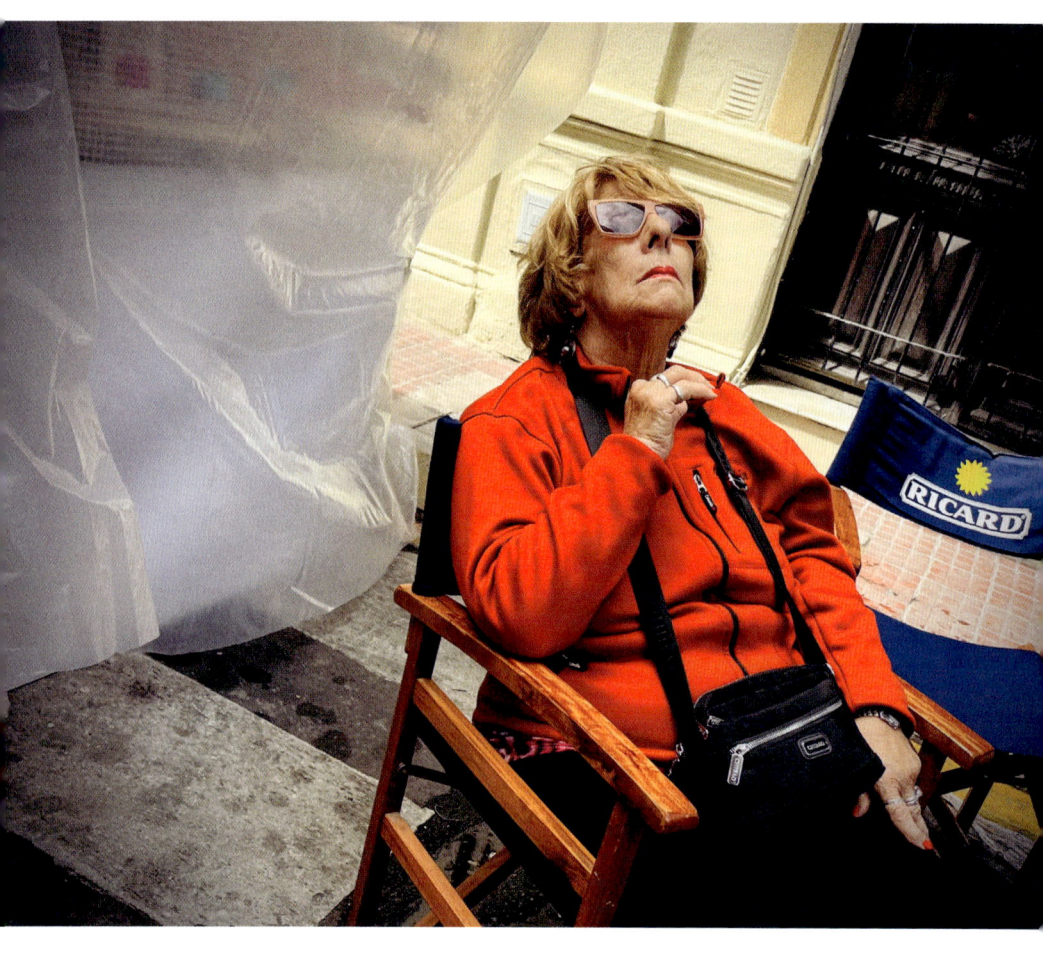

17. TAKE A PORTRAIT OF SOMEONE

PEOPLE ARE CENTRAL to classic street photography. It is obvious, as a face, a look or demeanour communicates something personal and unique. What you see is part of the setting, and you can capture them there and then. A street photographer can choose between shooting pictures anonymously or asking permission. The latter is more formal, but you get closer to your subject and can have a conversation you would not otherwise have. Look to Brandon Stanton, Tina Lodetti, Bruce Gilden and Dawoud Bey for inspiration. See also *May I Take Your Picture?* on page 72.

THERE IS NOTHING MORE INTERESTING THAN THE LANDSCAPE OF THE HUMAN FACE.

Irvin Kershner

18. LEAVE THE CITY

THE CITY IS the street photographer's home turf, but you should also visit other locations. Take the car, bus, train, or bike to the countryside. Walk in the woods, climb a hill or take the opportunity to visit a friend outside the city. Maybe you will open up new horizons by testing some landscape motifs. No doubt you will return with new images, and possibly a new perspective on what it means to photograph in city streets and squares.

VISIT THE COUNTRYSIDE

19. FOLLOW THE LIGHT

THE CITY CHANGES character depending on what time of day you venture out. *The golden hour* falls immediately after sunrise or an hour before sunset. It is characterised by a warm, often magical glow and long shadows (raking light). If you take your pictures at mid-day, and there are no clouds, you have to work with sharp contrast and strong colours, which is not something everyone enjoys. Read more about photographing in the evening and at night on pages 71 and 110.

PHOTOGRAPH AT DAWN OR DUSK

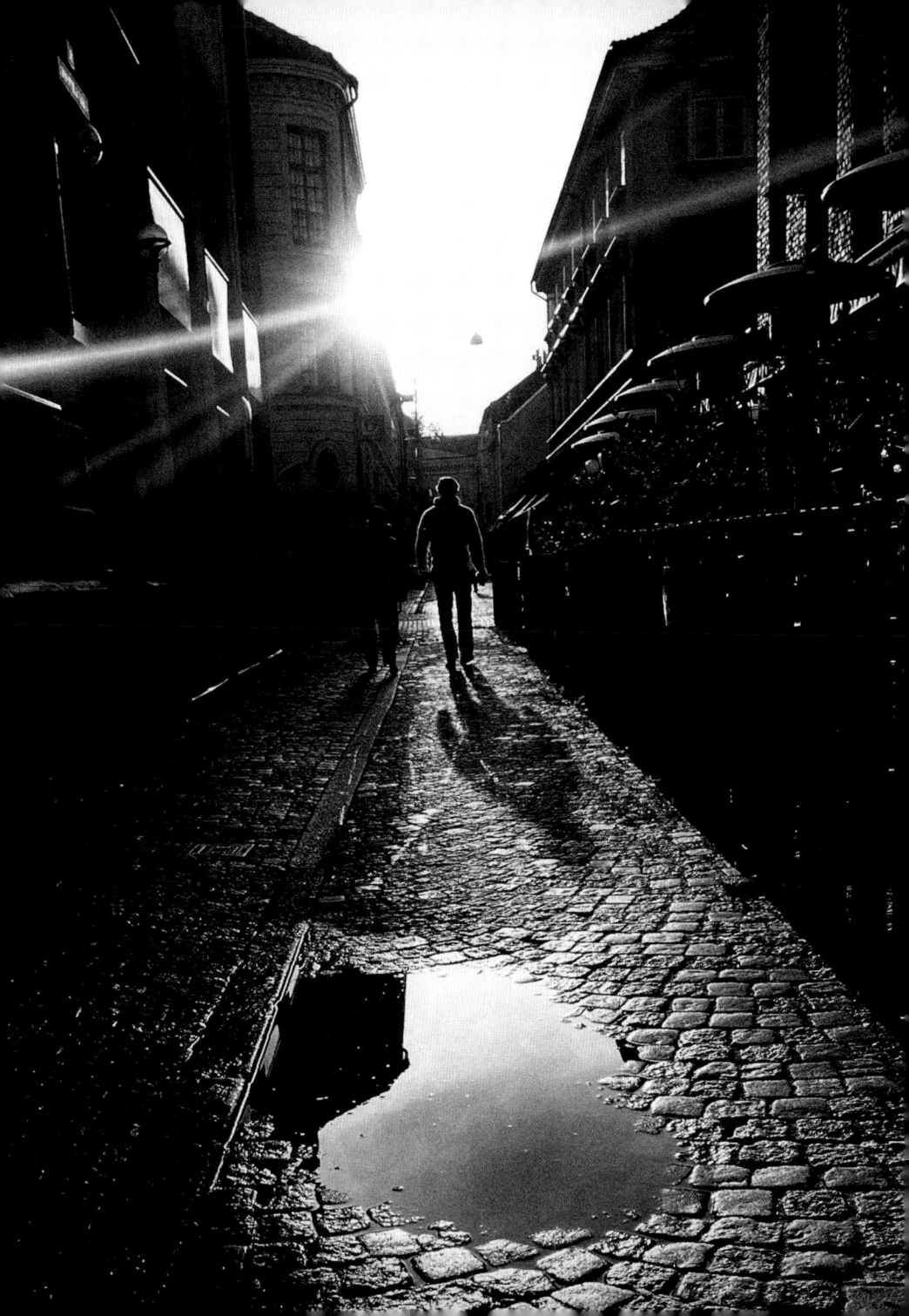

20. GET TO KNOW YOUR PREJUDICES

STEREOTYPES EXIST everywhere, also within street photography. It means that we observe the world according to our prejudices. Stereotypes can make it easier to interpret the world around us, but often they feed prejudices and misinterpretations by simplifying and reducing information. We all have them; it is a good idea to sometimes consider our choices in terms of motif. What kind of pictures reinforce stereotypes? Who might question them? What are your prejudices? Use your camera to get to know others, and yourself.

CHALLENGE YOUR IMAGE SENSE
– TAKE A PICTURE THAT
CHALLENGES A PREJUDICE

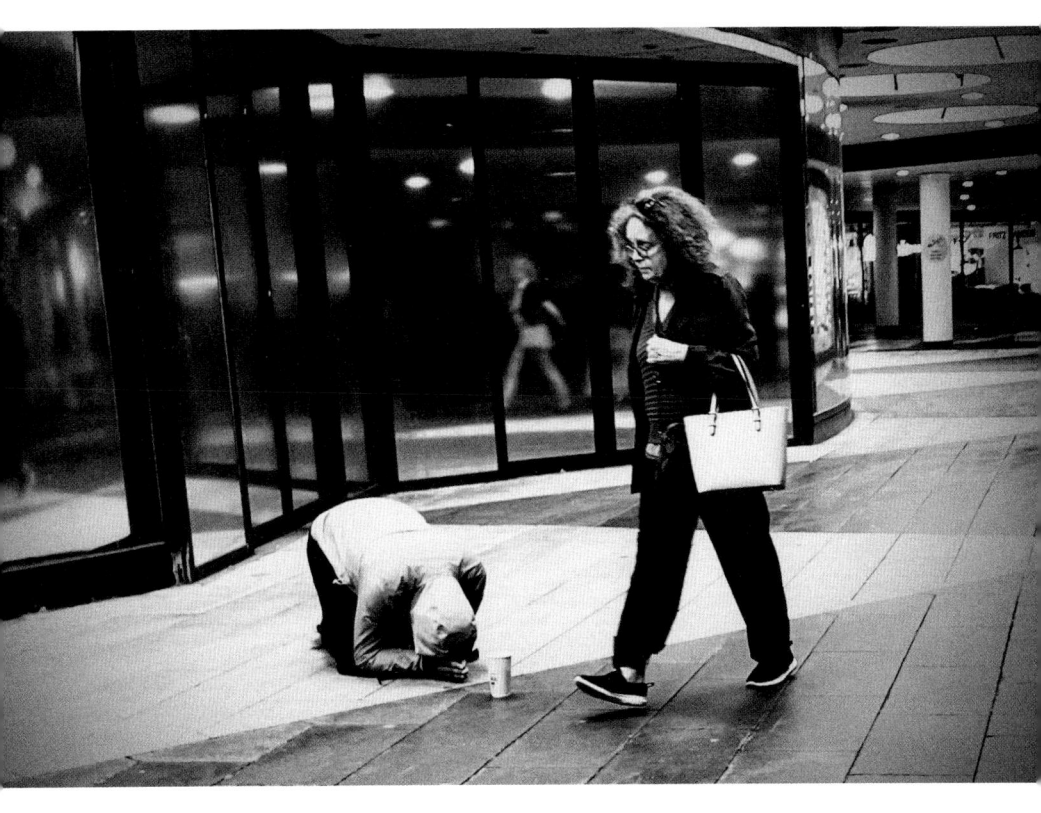

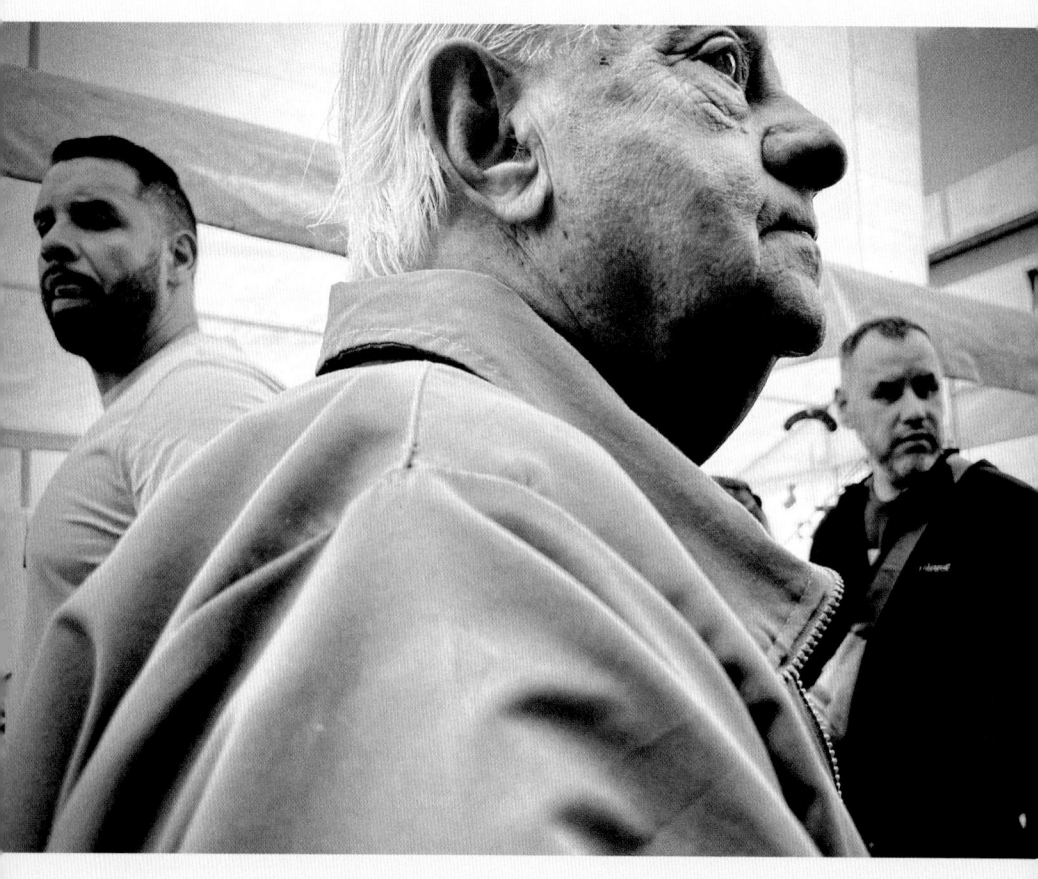

21. TAKE A CHANCE

LEAVE IT UP to chance. Do not overthink; follow your mood, feelings and intuition. Your pictures are guaranteed to come out differently. The city offers many angles, maybe you will find your own by not over-planning. The method is not unlike *shooting from the hip*, as you will not be looking into the viewfinder. There is no risk of bothering people around you, and your pictures will turn out less arranged. Some of them will be unusable, but you will also find personal, emotional and unexpected interpretations of street life.

SOMETIMES, I'D TAKE SHOTS WITHOUT AIMING,
JUST TO SEE WHAT HAPPENED.
I'D RUSH INTO CROWDS
– BANG! BANG!...
IT MUST BE CLOSE TO WHAT A FIGHTER FEELS AFTER
JABBING AND CIRCLING AND GETTING HIT,
WHEN SUDDENLY THERE IS AN OPENING,
AND BANG!
RIGHT ON THE BUTTON.
IT IS A FANTASTIC FEELING.

William Klein

CLOSE YOUR EYES AND GO FOR IT

22. BE A TOURIST

STREET PHOTOGRAPHERS would hardly like to see others comparing their pictures to tourist snapshots. To be where everyone else is and take pictures that look like existing pictures is counterintuitive to the idea of them being spontaneous and authentic. But you can make a point by breaking with this snobbery and make your own variations of holiday snapshots. The word "tourist" derives from the Latin tornare, which means twisting, turning, orbiting. Interesting motifs can often be found, but perhaps from a different perspective, which is something Martin Parr has used. Why not become a tourist in your own neighbourhood?

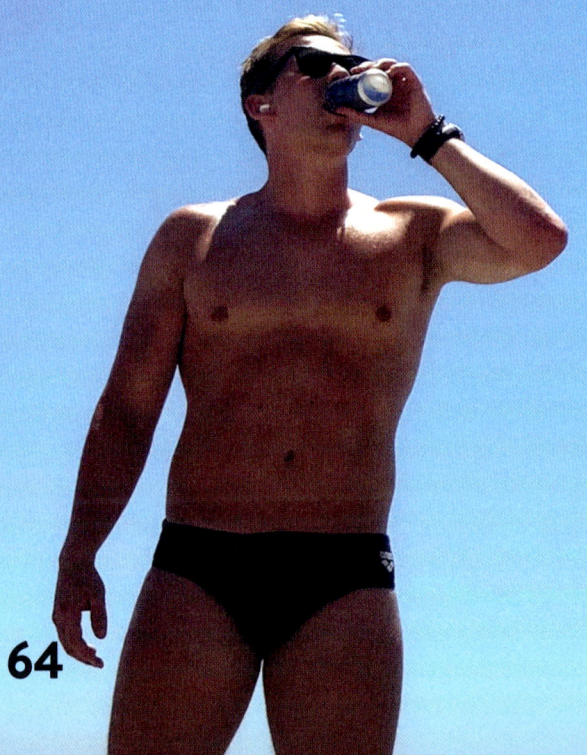
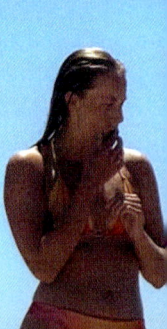

TAKE PICTURES WHERE EVERYONE ELSE TAKES PICTURES

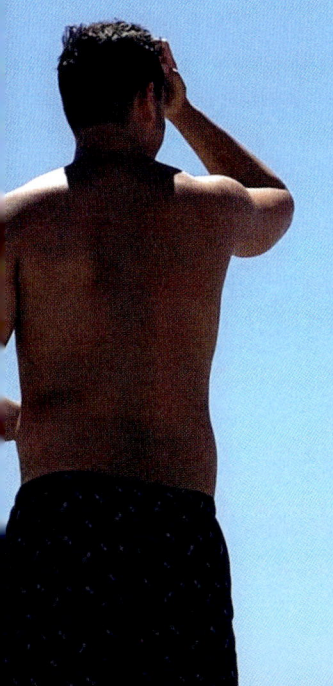

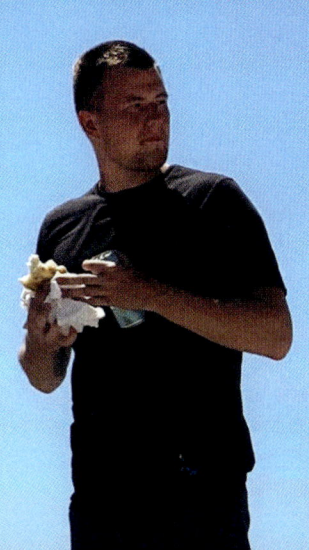

23. MAKE A PHOTO REPORTAGE

BY DESCRIBING SOMETHING via a series of interconnected pictures you allow for more complex, in-depth narratives in which you can focus on an emotion, a development or an event. There are no templates to follow, but it is a good idea to look for inspiration offered by some photojournalists that have attracted an international audience in a way that would not have been possible using only words: Dorothea Lange (Migrant Mother), Carol Guzy (Kosovo's Sorrow), James Nachtwey (9/11 Series) and W. Eugene Smith (Country Doctor). Are you still stuck on taking individual pictures? Think like a film director. What scenes would you need to compose an interesting story?

MAKE A PHOTO REPORTAGE
WITH FIVE PICTURES ABOUT _____

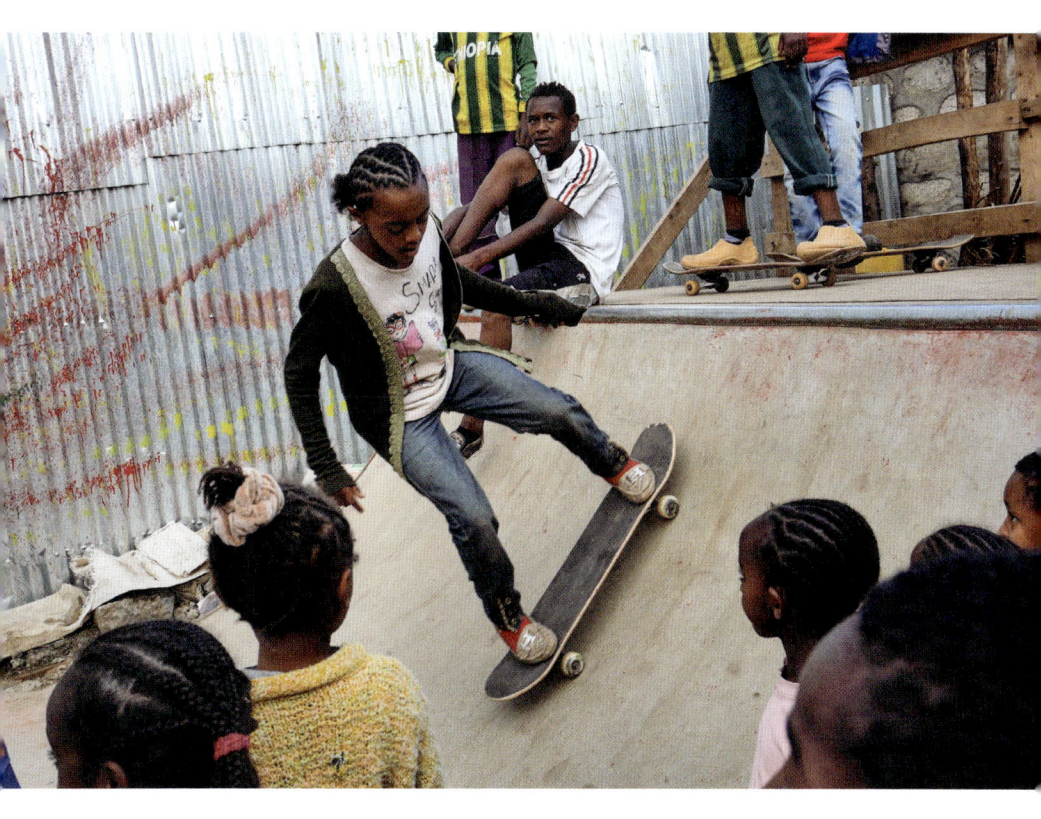

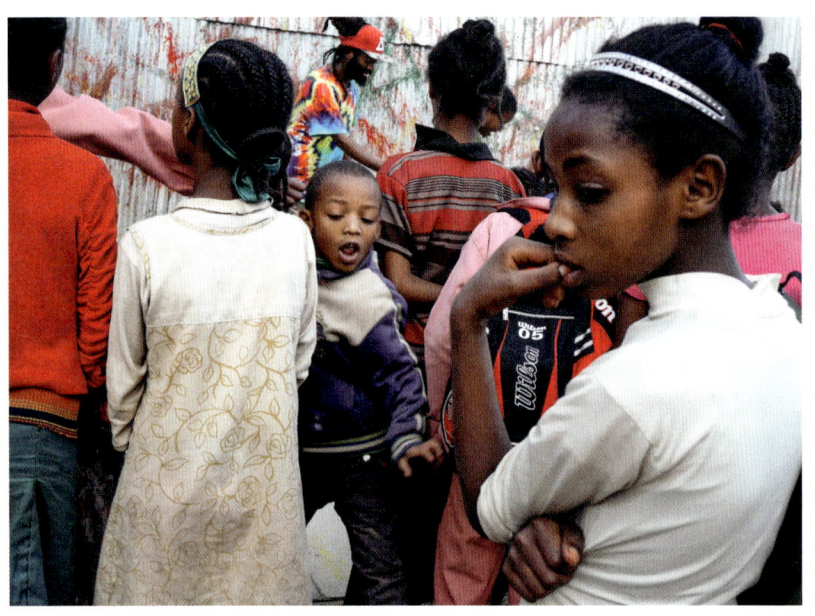

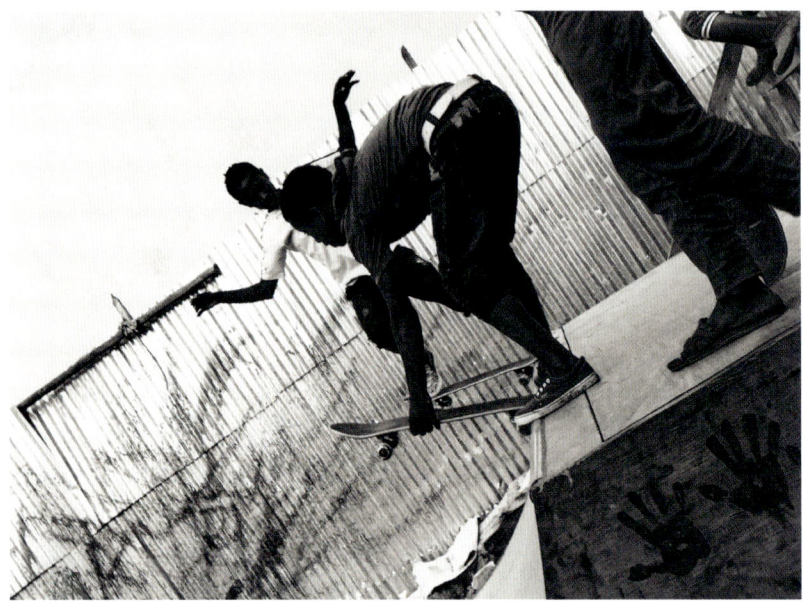

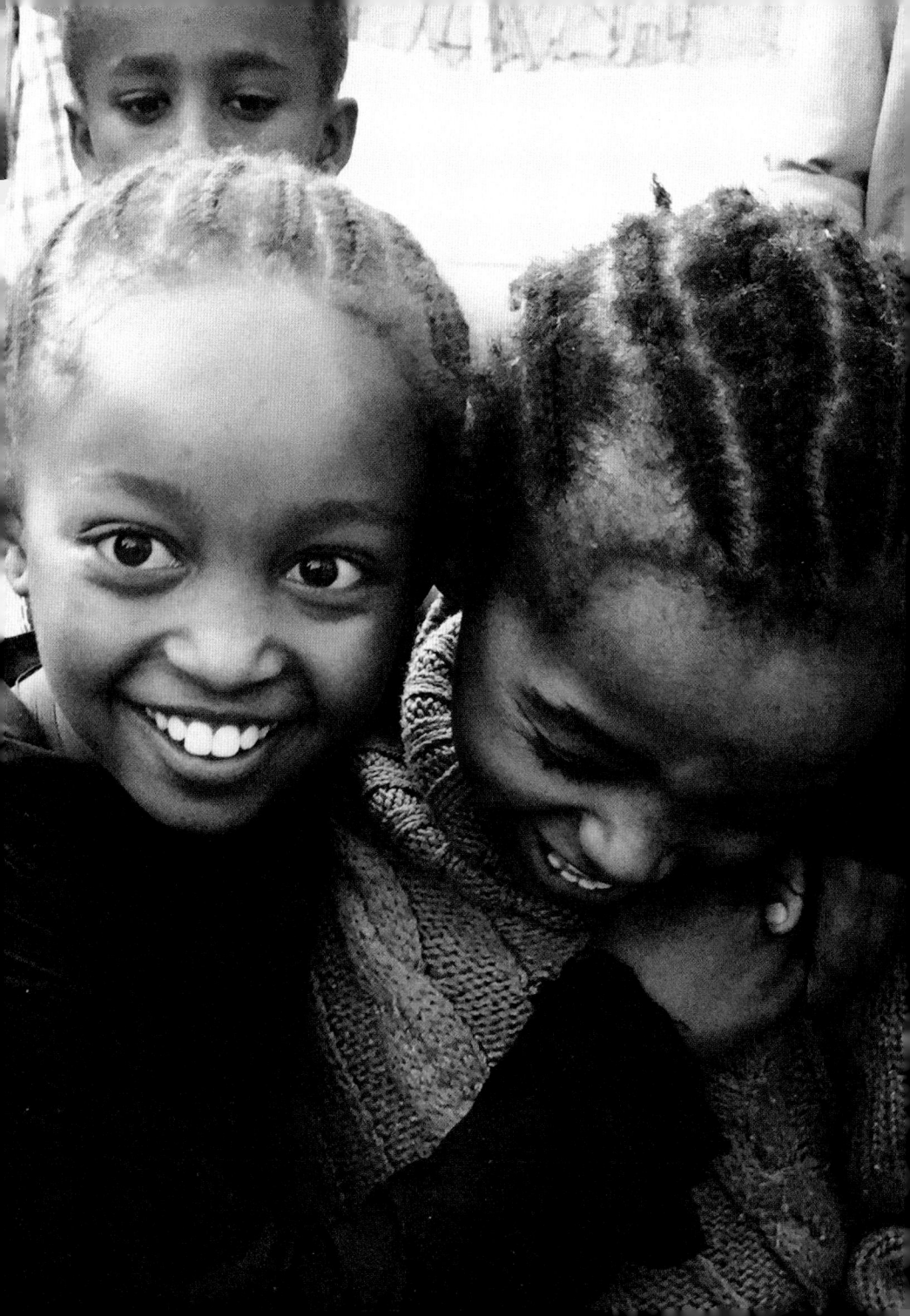

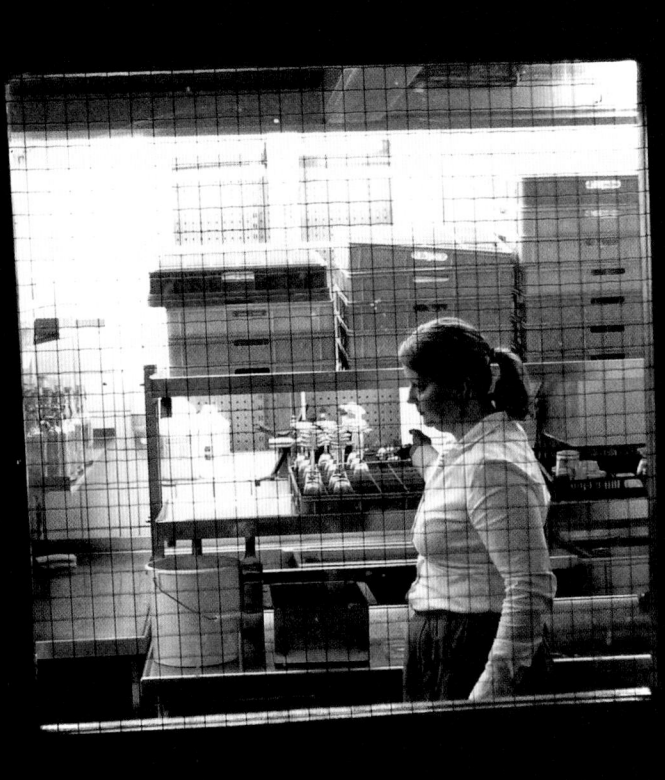

24. BECOME A NOCTURNAL ANIMAL

VENTURING OUT AT night is both exciting and challenging. You soon discover that you need to reconsider much of the work you have done before as you constantly need to be aware of how to use light. A nocturnal photographer often works with a suitable lens, aperture and ISO setting, and the right shutter times. Or completely ignore all of this. Atmosphere and presence are often more interesting than perfect lighting conditions. So, be creative: your palette now consists of shadows, reflections and light sources such as shop windows, neon signs and streetlights. The reward is that you encounter the city in a guise consisting of grey scales, blackness and contrast. You can be anonymous in the dark, but always be aware of your surroundings when you are out at night.

*UGLY AND GREY DURING THE DAY,
A CITY BECOMES ATTRACTIVE AT NIGHT.*

Patrick Zachmann

EMBRACE THE DARK –
PHOTOGRAPH AT NIGHT

25. MAY I TAKE YOUR PICTURE?

MEET NEW PEOPLE by stopping and talking to someone you would like to photograph. Everyone is not as easy to engage in conversation, but a few words suffice for people to overcome the suspicion that often arises when you are out photographing in the street. You are often met with appreciation when you explain what you are doing. A smile helps. Show them the pictures and offer to send them copies as a gift. Exploit a person's curiosity and tell them why you like to walk around taking pictures, but never intrude on their privacy.

SAY "MAY I TAKE A
PHOTOGRAPH OF YOU"
TO FIVE PEOPLE IN ONE DAY

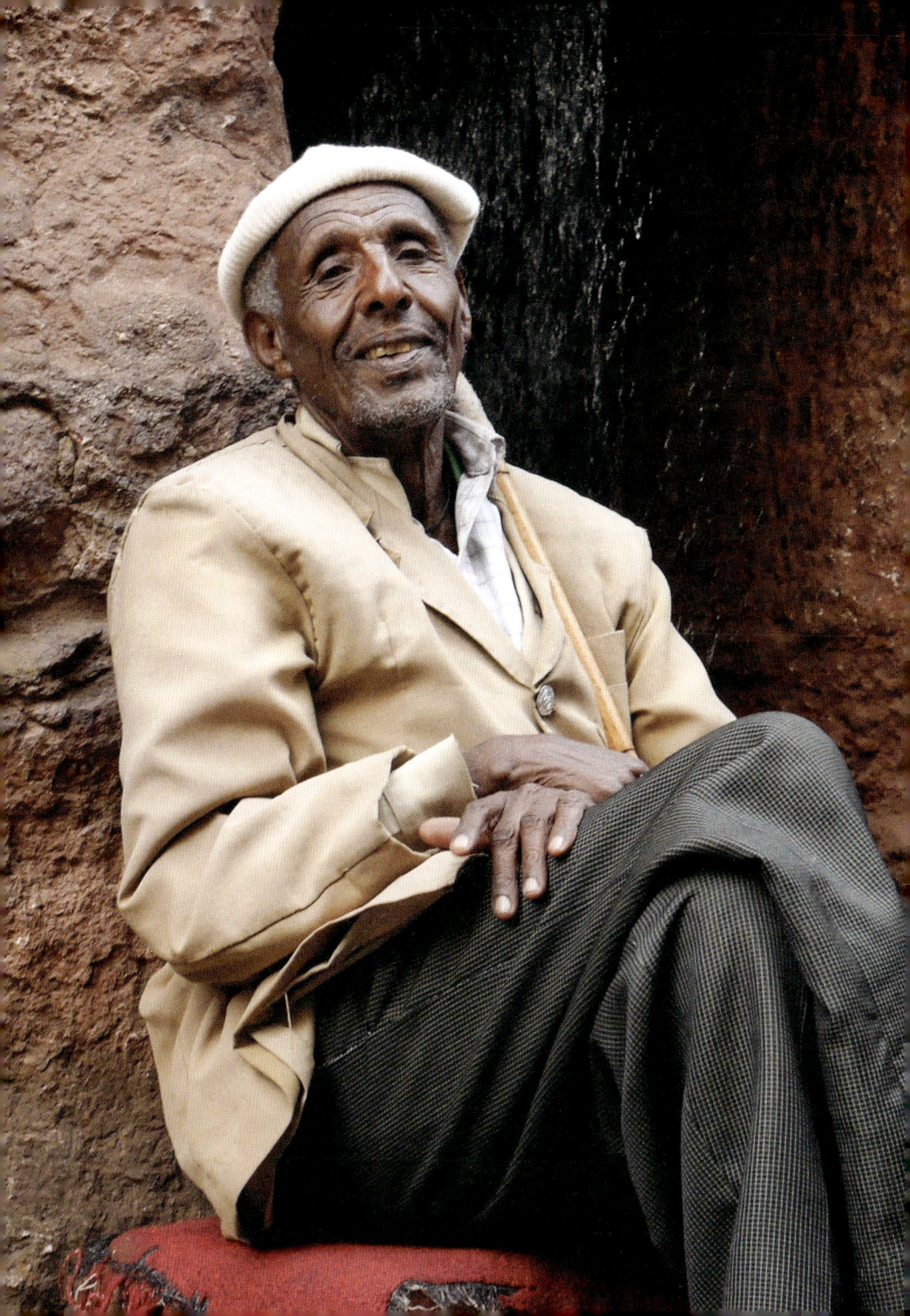

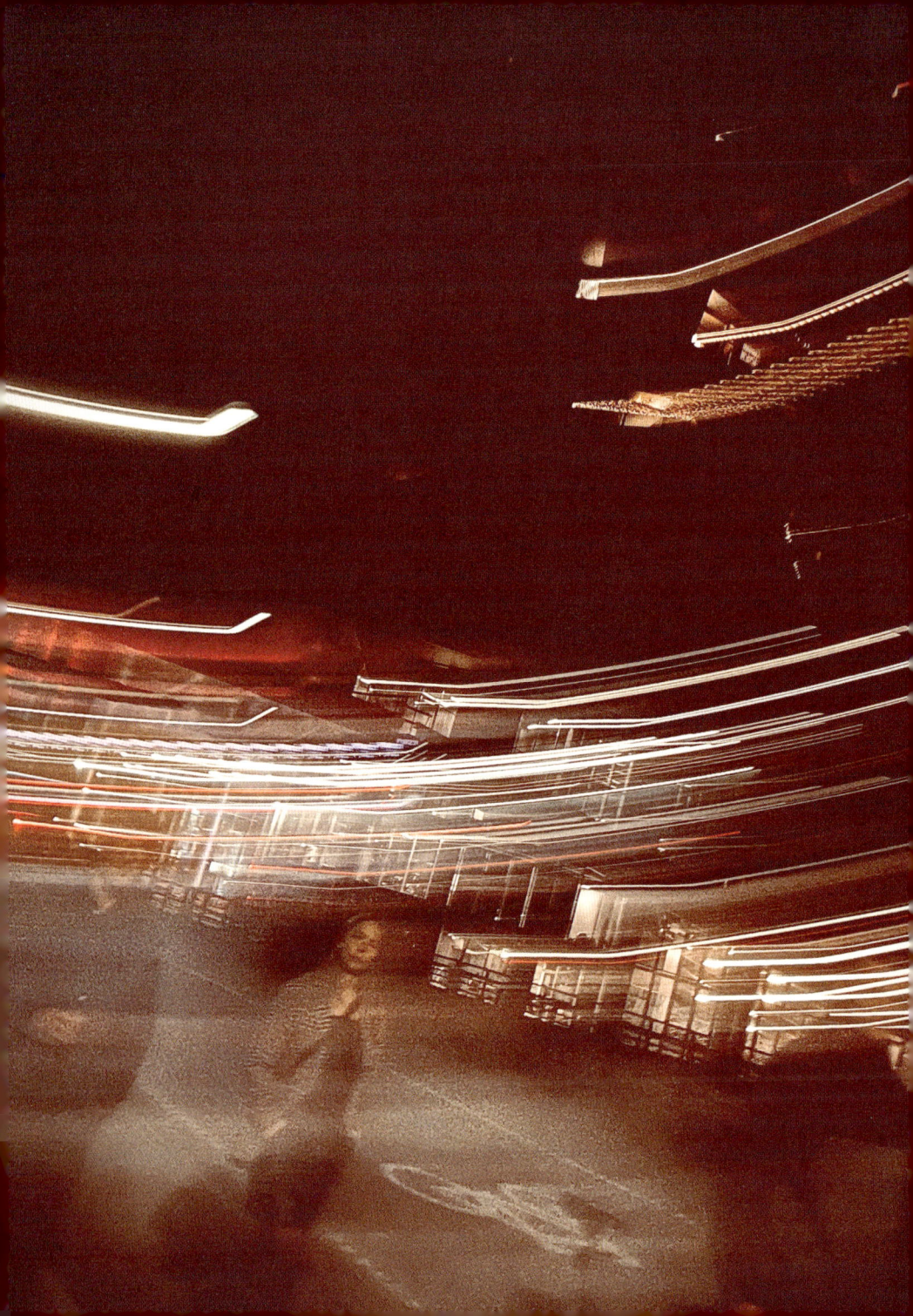

26. BE ABSTRACT

SOME ARE LOOKING for realism, others want to explore the unclear and abstract. Abstract photography is a popular form of street photography that allows for playfulness and experimentation. It gives you the freedom to break with norms and make use of reflections, shadows, textures, silhouettes and raindrops on windows, or capture reflections in water and on wet streets. You can blur large areas (so-called *bokeh photography*). Over the years, Saul Leiter, a pioneer within the genre, has created a fascinating, surrealist world filled with distortions and blur.

A WINDOW COVERED WITH RAINDROPS INTERESTS ME MORE THAN A PHOTOGRAPH OF A FAMOUS PERSON.
Saul Leiter

27. GO WHERE NO ONE ELSE GOES

THROUGH URBAN EXPLORATION, urbex, you explore parts of the city that are abandoned or hidden. It is similar to street photography, but in this case, you look for uninhabited houses, tunnels or closed-down factories with the purpose of documenting hidden places and their history. There is a code that says you must leave the site untouched. Subgenres include terraces, indoor swimming pools and religious buildings. Do not forget that you always need to be aware of any safety risks and legal issues.

PHOTOGRAPH IN AN ABANDONED
CITY LOCATION

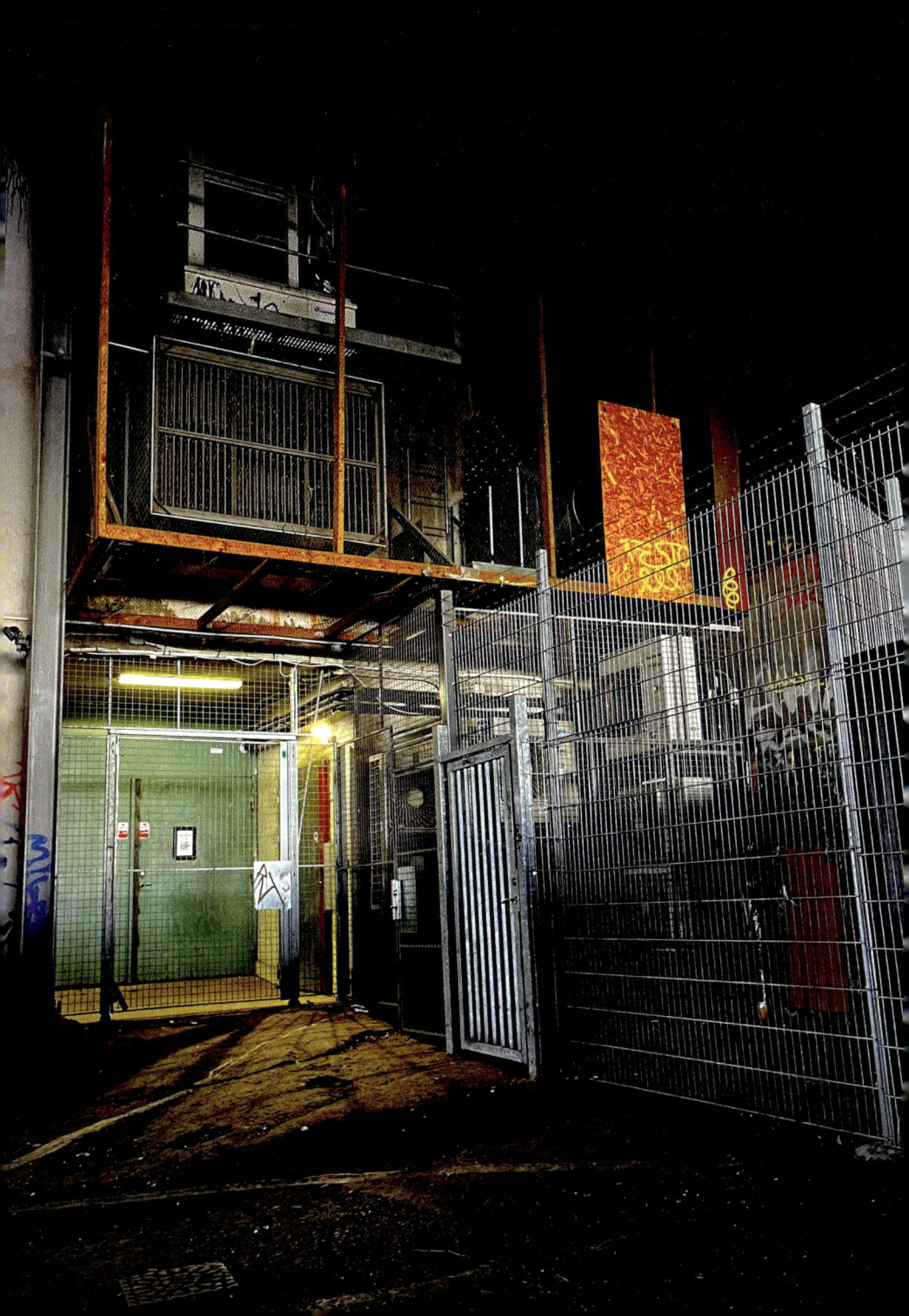

28. PLAY PHOTO BINGO

WHEN YOU ARE unable to come up with any ideas at all, it is time to bring out your street photo bingo. Make list of motifs you have to locate in an hour, day or week. Go out and try to tick them off as quickly as you can. Why not challenge a friend? Categories may include:

- Old doors
- Joggers or outdoor gyms
- Something broken
- Bridges
- Something oval
- Letters
- Graffiti

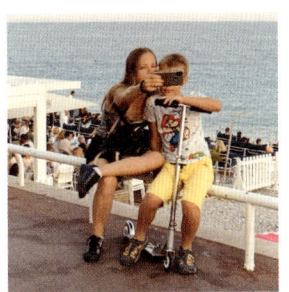 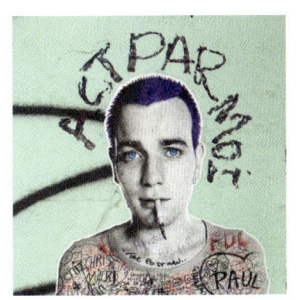 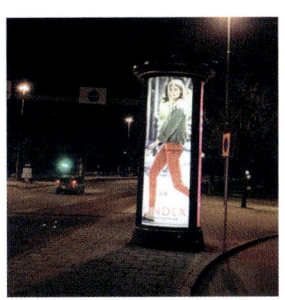

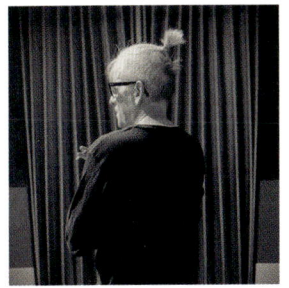 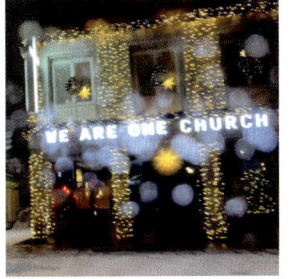 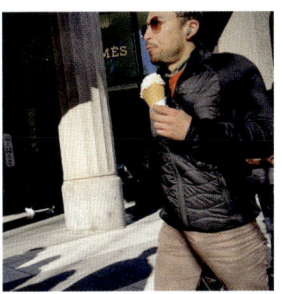

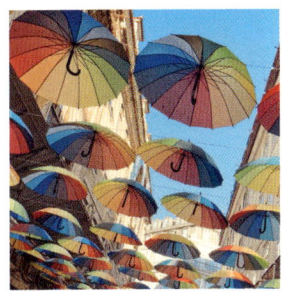 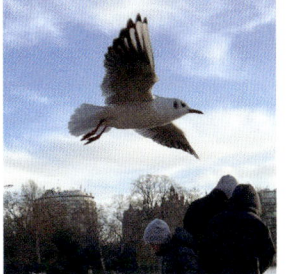 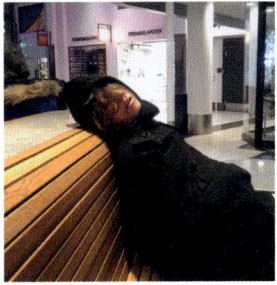

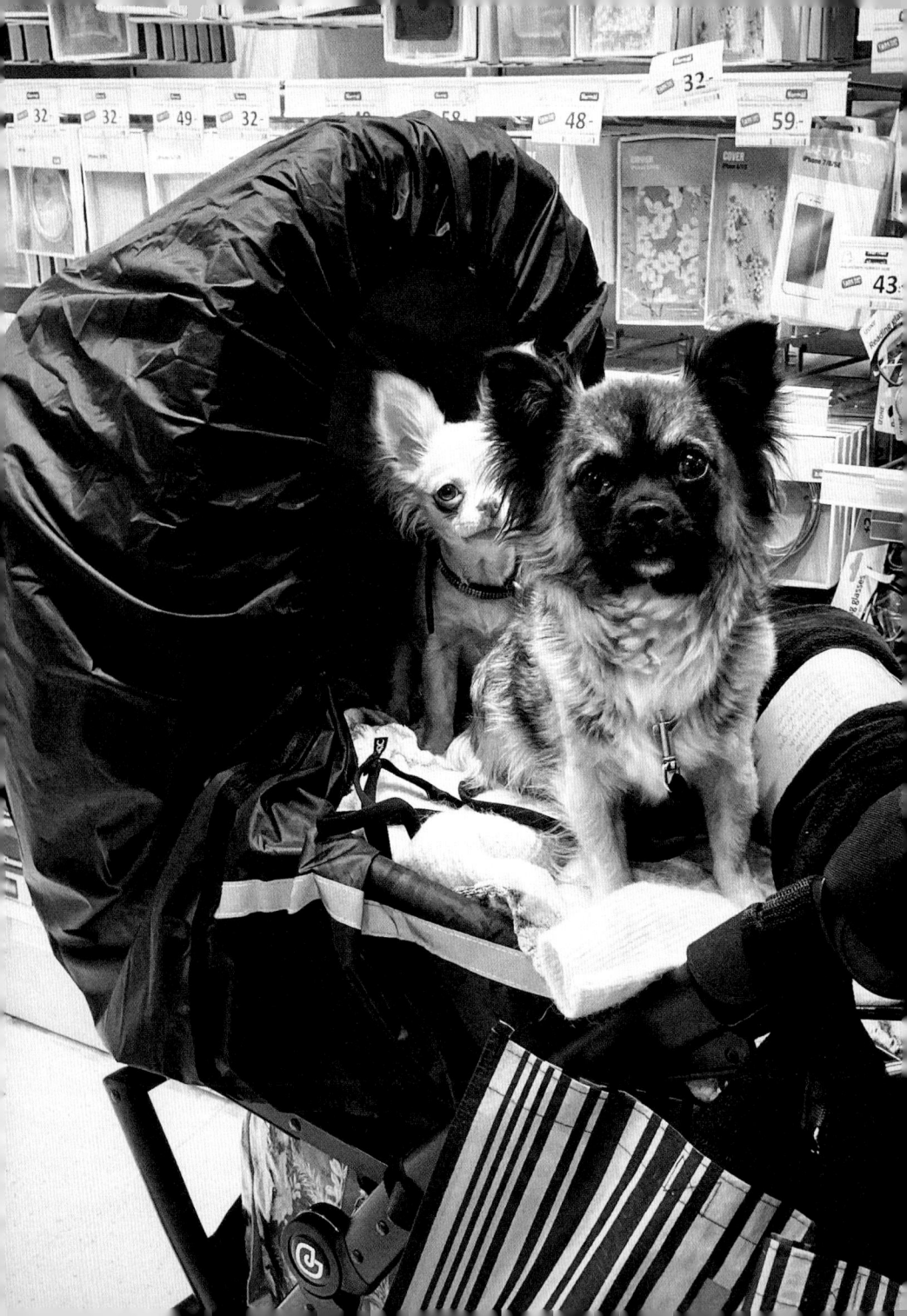

29. CATS AND DOGS ...

MOST PEOPLE WOULD agree that there is no lack of pictures of cute pets in the city. These are, together with people in front of advertising boards and people kissing, some of the most stereotypical motifs in street photography. But we also know that many of the most iconic examples of the genre are variations of this. Photographing animals can be a fun way of testing new settings, angles and contexts.

TAKE A PICTURE OF A DOG OR CAT IN AN UNEXPECTED SITUATION. OR INTRODUCE A DAY WHEN YOU ONLY PHOTOGRAPH ANIMALS.

30. ... AND CHILDREN

MANY OF THE most iconic pictures of children were taken in the street. William Klein, Steve McCurry, Helen Levitt and many others have portrayed the lives of children and young people in cities. Today, taking spontaneous photographs of children has become contentious. People are more suspicious, which is why it is often avoided. There is concern about how these pictures will be spread. At the same time, it would be strange for a street photographer not to photograph children in the streets. So do continue, but make it relevant and respectful.

DO PHOTOGRAPH CHILDREN (BUT ASK THEIR PARENTS FIRST)

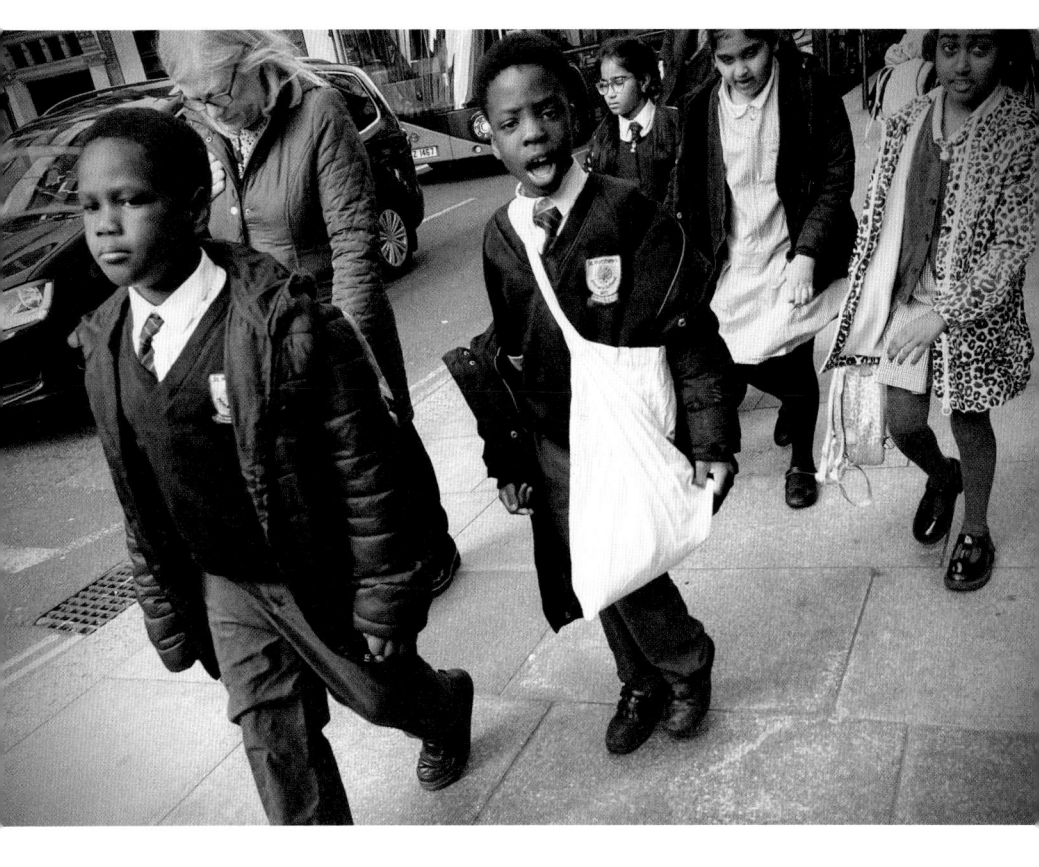

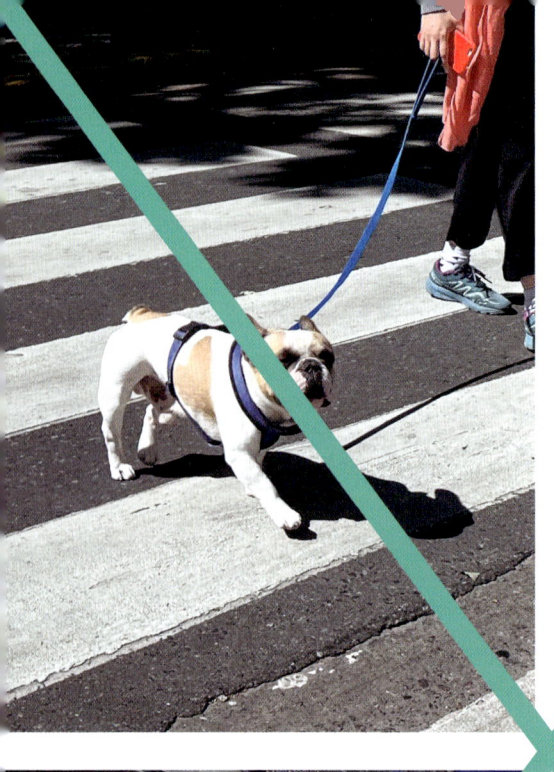
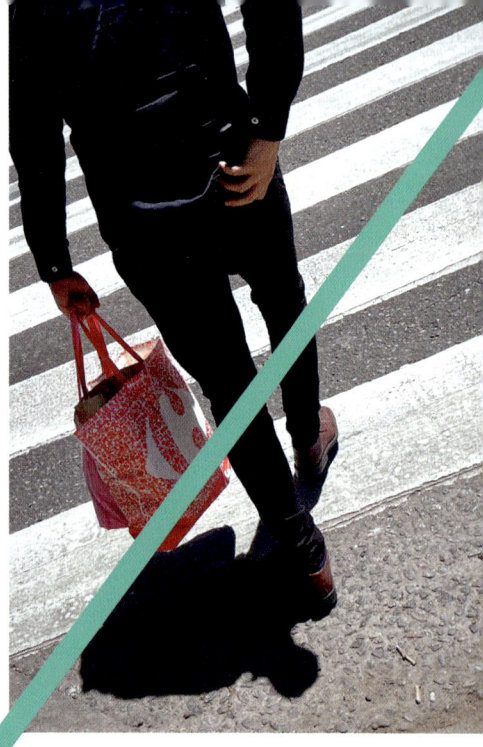
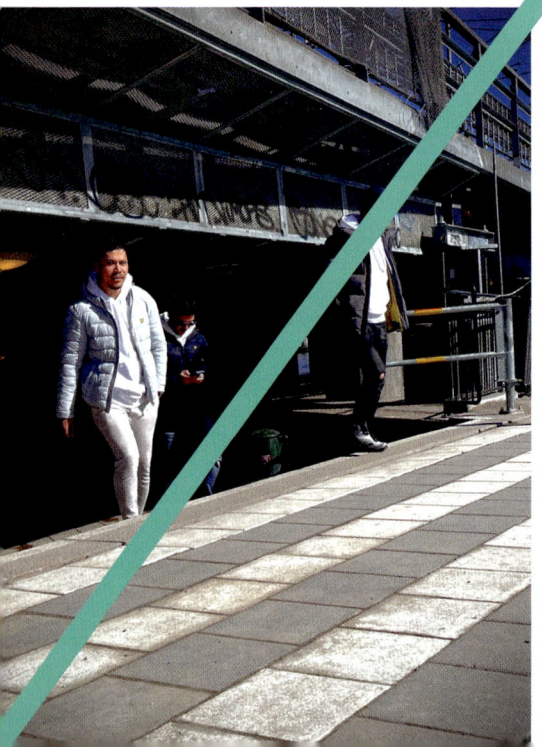
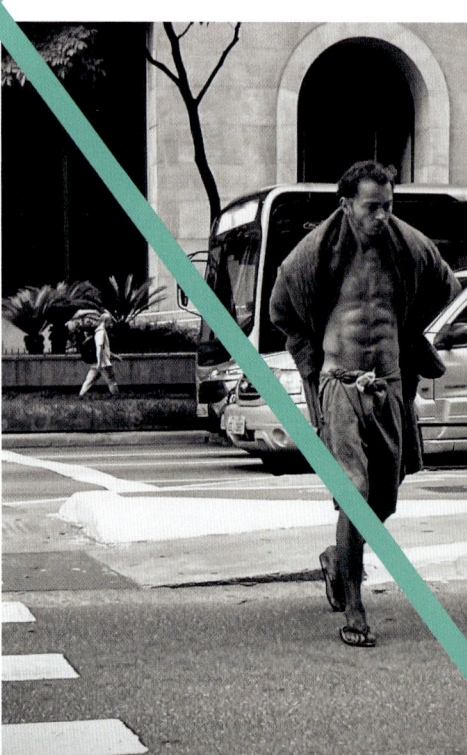

31. KILL YOUR DARLINGS

"kill your darlings" is about paring down content and focusing on what is most important. In a text, you might choose to edit out formulations you like, but that complicate the message for the reader. Film makers might remove a character that is interesting, but that does not fit into the narrative arc. In photography, you need to take a moment to question the most hackneyed solutions. Killing your darlings may be hard (I somehow manage to include pedestrian crossings in my pictures). The issue comes up when you need to make a selection. It is a good idea to make an initial selection and then leave it to the following day. Another is to ask someone you trust or show your pictures without revealing who took them.

- Pick a series of pictures
- Which are your favourites?
- Do they add to your message?
- Remove the ones that do not
- Compare before and after
- Ask a friend to look at the result

*KILL YOUR DARLINGS, KILL YOUR DARLINGS,
EVEN WHEN IT BREAKS YOUR EGOCENTRIC
LITTLE SCRIBBLER'S HEART,
KILL YOUR DARLINGS.*

Stephen King

32. TELL YOUR STORY

AS A STREET PHOTOGRAPHER you are free to create any story you want, even if it is related to your own life. You are part of the city, and you should allow your personal impressions, thoughts and emotions to inform your work. What has influenced you? Are there places that have a special meaning to you? What does your old school look like today? Do not be afraid of using your own experiences, they are unique and may be more interesting than you thought to begin with.

EVERYBODY HAS AS STORY TO TELL.

Joe Strummer

VISIT A PLACE THAT MEANS A LOT TO YOU

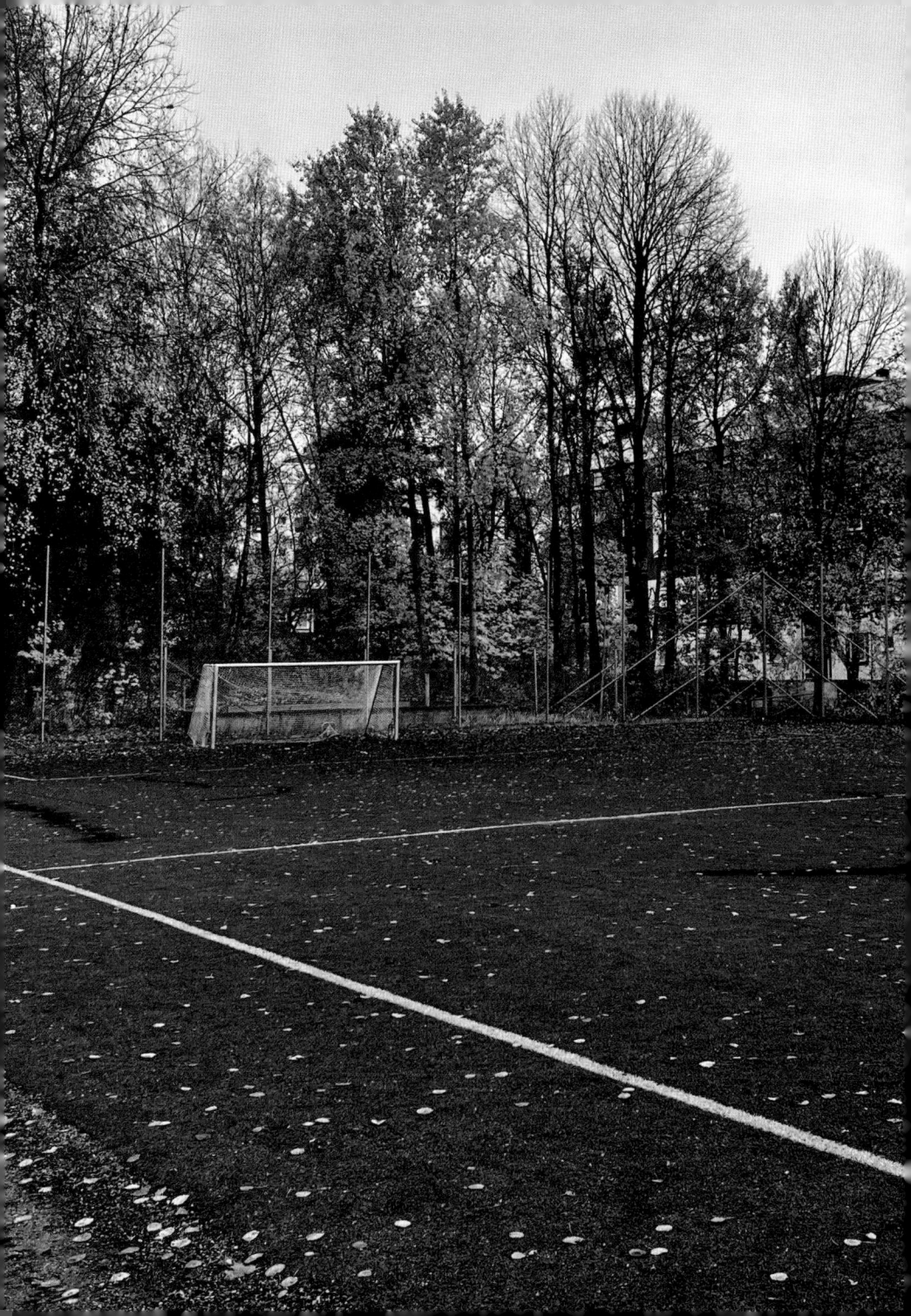

33. DO A 360 TURN

MAKE IT A HABIT to make a full circle turn. It offers you a general view of the setting, and you will discover new angles and more light sources.

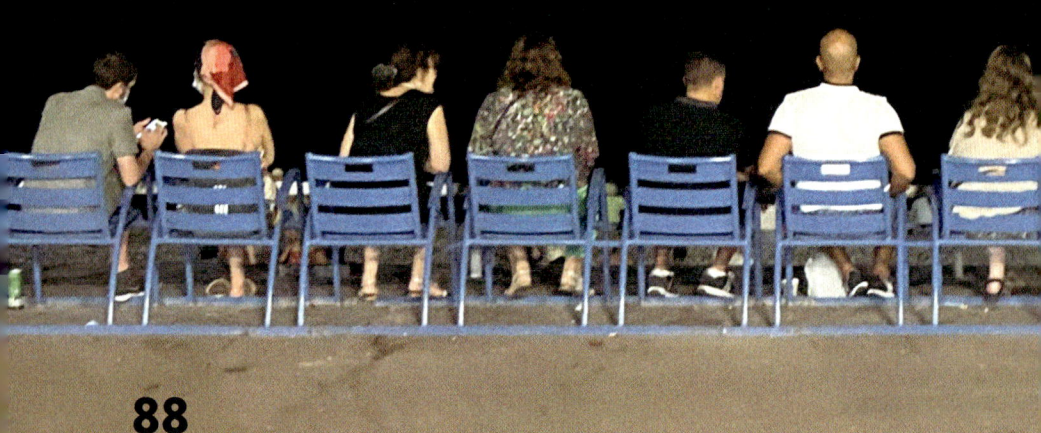

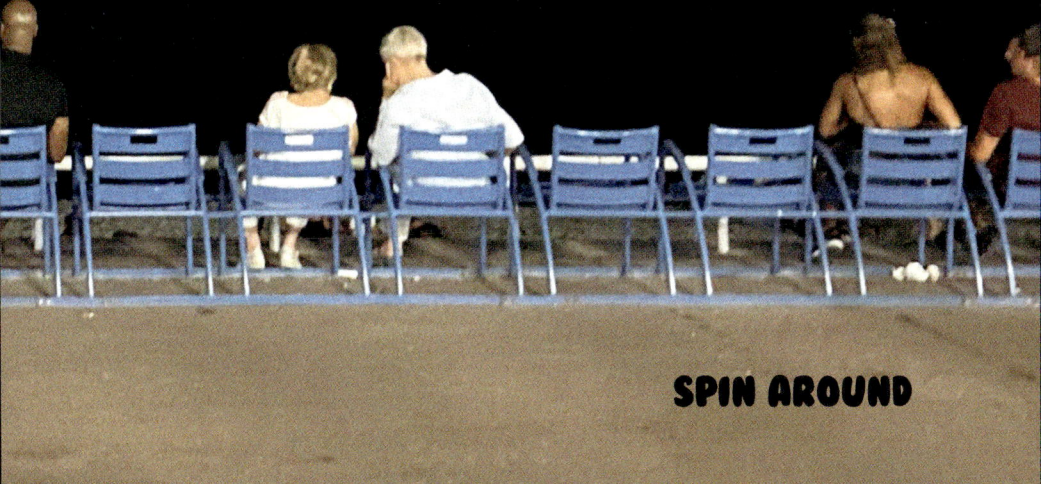

SPIN AROUND

34. REPEAT YOURSELF

YOU CAN ACHIEVE structure and motivation by repeating yourself from time to time. Take pictures of a street, a bus stop, or a building at a precise time. Or participate in an a-picture-a-day *photo challenge*. You could document something once a month or once a year. These are only a few examples of how to use numbers to guide your creative process. Over a period of nine years, Danish photographer Peter Funch photographed people on their way to work from exactly the same spot.

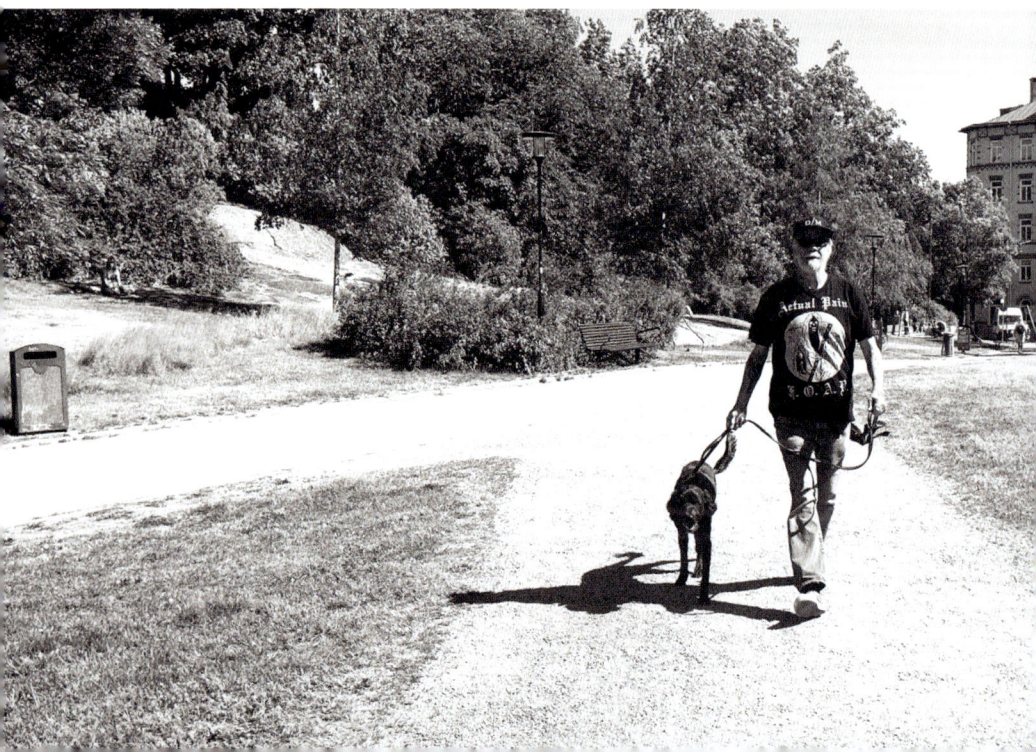

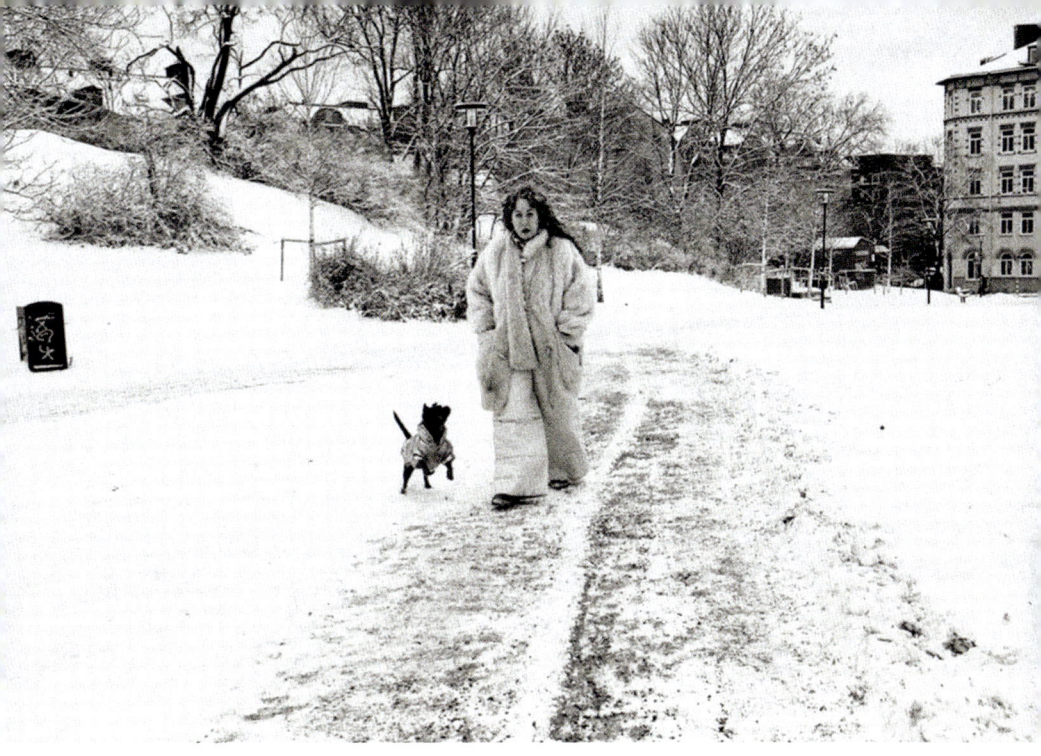

Martin Parr

PHOTOGRAPH THE SAME
MOTIF X TIMES

35. EMULATE A MASTER

WHO ARE YOUR favourite photographers? If you study them closely and copy their work diligently you will become as good as they are. Not! No one wants to appear like a copycat, and you obviously need to discover your own style. But getting there can go via role models. How did they go about making those photos that you and so many others admire? You will soon discover that it is almost impossible to recreate a photography. Hopefully, you will realise it if you have been too inspired by a master. No favourites? Have a look at Garry Winogrand, Lee Friedlander and Daido Moriyama.

STEAL LIKE AN ARTIST.
Austin Kleon

COPY YOUR FAVOURITE
PHOTOGRAPHER

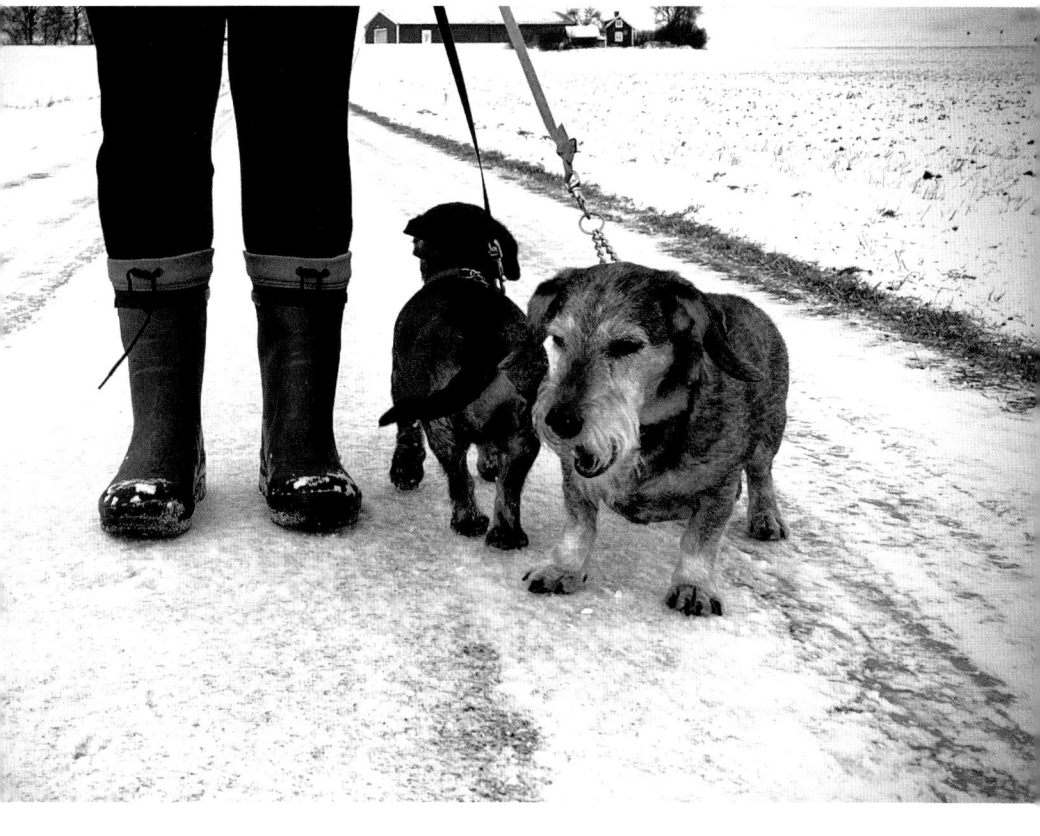

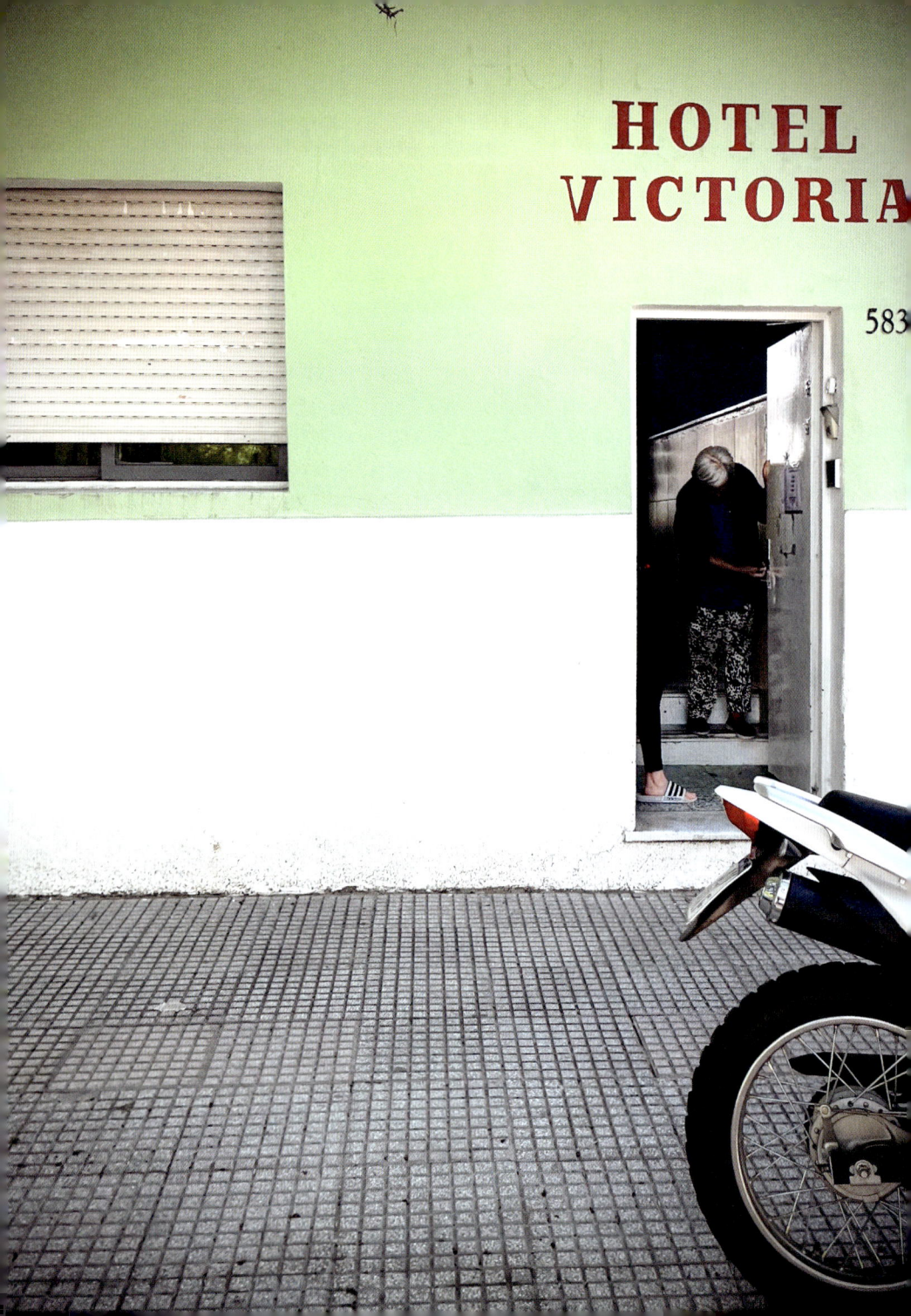

36. CHALLENGE YOURSELF

CHALLENGES ARE HARD, but they are also important to your creative development. You often need to break a habit and remove yourself from your comfort zone. As a street photographer you might want to think about what feels hard or uncomfortable. Could it be fear of failing? Do you lack time or resources? It is generally a question of looking for new settings or other ways of taking photographs. Have there been occasions you could have dealt with differently? It is time to tread where you previously feared to tread.

MOST PEOPLE ONLY TAKE SNAPSHOTS OF THINGS IMMEDIATELY AROUND THEM IN THEIR DAILY LIFE. FUNDAMENTALLY THAT MEANS THAT THEY'RE NOT GOING OUT OF THEIR COMFORT ZONE. BUT OUT ON THE CITY STREETS, EVERYTHING YOU ENCOUNTER IS ALIEN AND UNKNOWN. THAT IS WHAT TAKING SNAPSHOT PHOTOGRAPHS OF THE CITY STREETS IS: YOU'RE CAPTURING THE ALIEN AND UNKNOWN.

Daido Moriyama

TAKE PICTURES WHERE IT FEELS UNCOMFORTABLE

37. TAKE FEWER PICTURES

DIGITAL PHOTOGRAPHY offers many advantages to street photographers, but with limitless storage comes the risk of becoming lazy and less attentive. You routinely shoot pictures thinking that "at least one should be good". One way of counteracting this is to take fewer pictures. With an analogue camera, you can take no more than 24 or 36. The purpose is to focus on situations that offer the most interesting motifs.

TAKE NO MORE THAN 24 PICTURES
IN A DAY. OR ONE – ONLY ONE –
A DAY FOR A WEEK

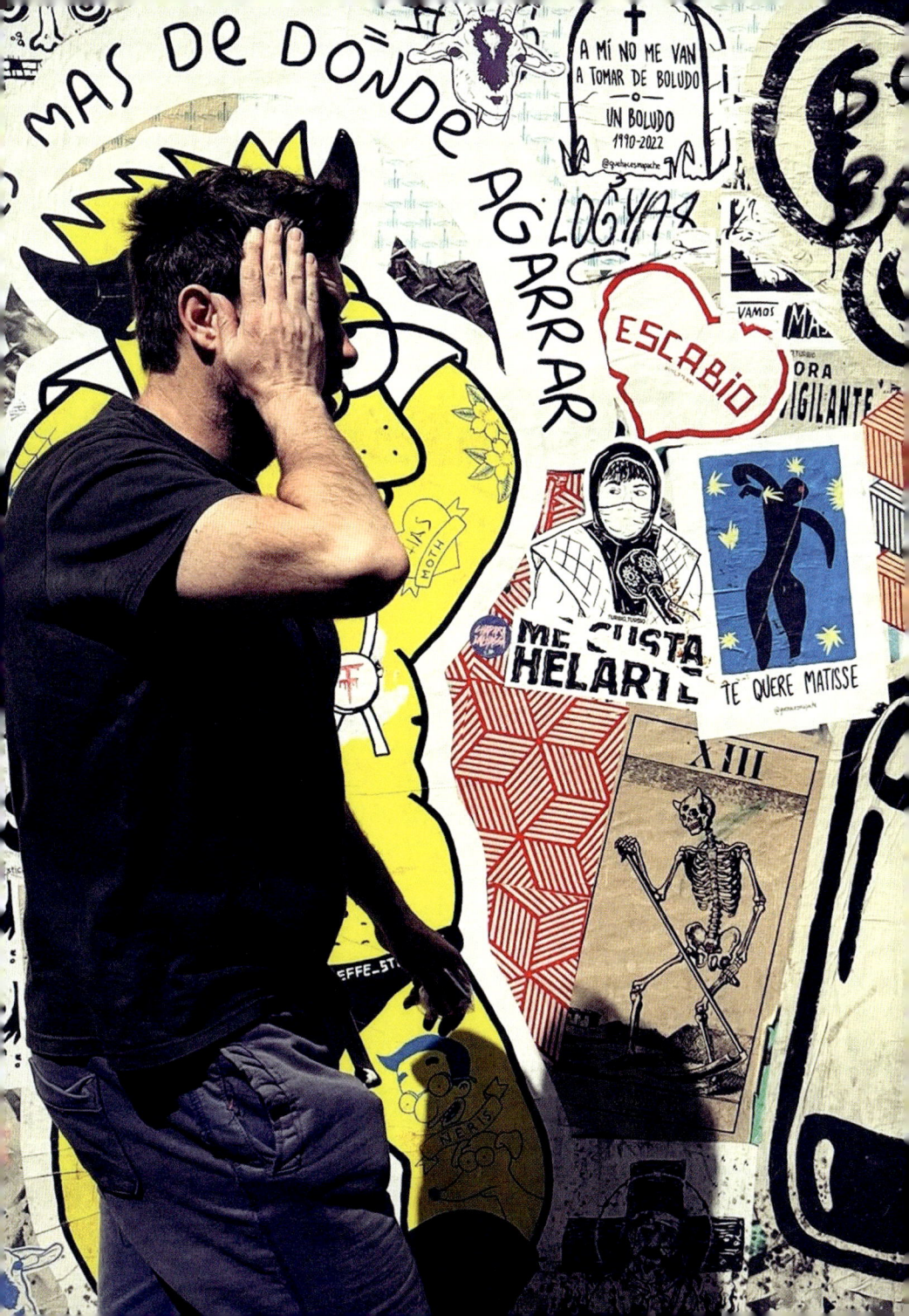

38. THINK BIG

IT HAS BEEN said that a wild imagination opens the door to creativity. So why not aim a little higher – go for it! Think of haute couture, an expression of the highest possible standard within fashion and design. By starting with a great vision, you avoid getting trapped in everyday musts and problems. So, stand up straight, dream and do not think about any obstacles. You may not reach absolute perfection, but you will develop your creativity.

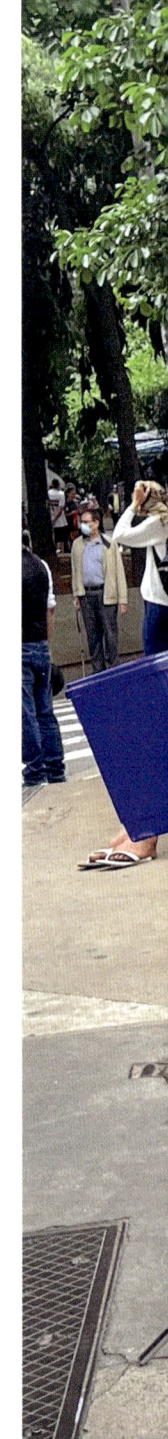

**MAKE YOUR PHOTO
DREAM COME TRUE**

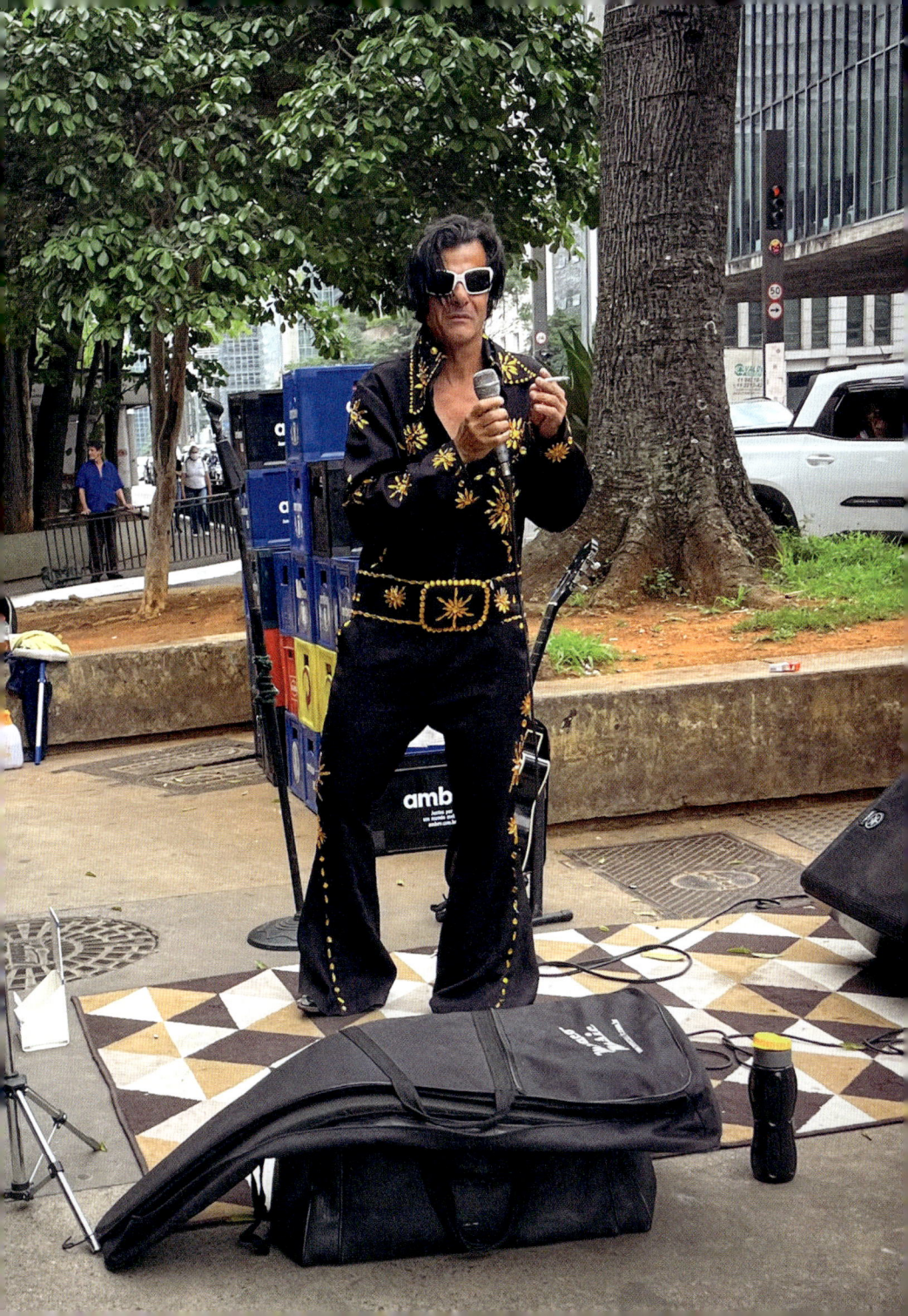

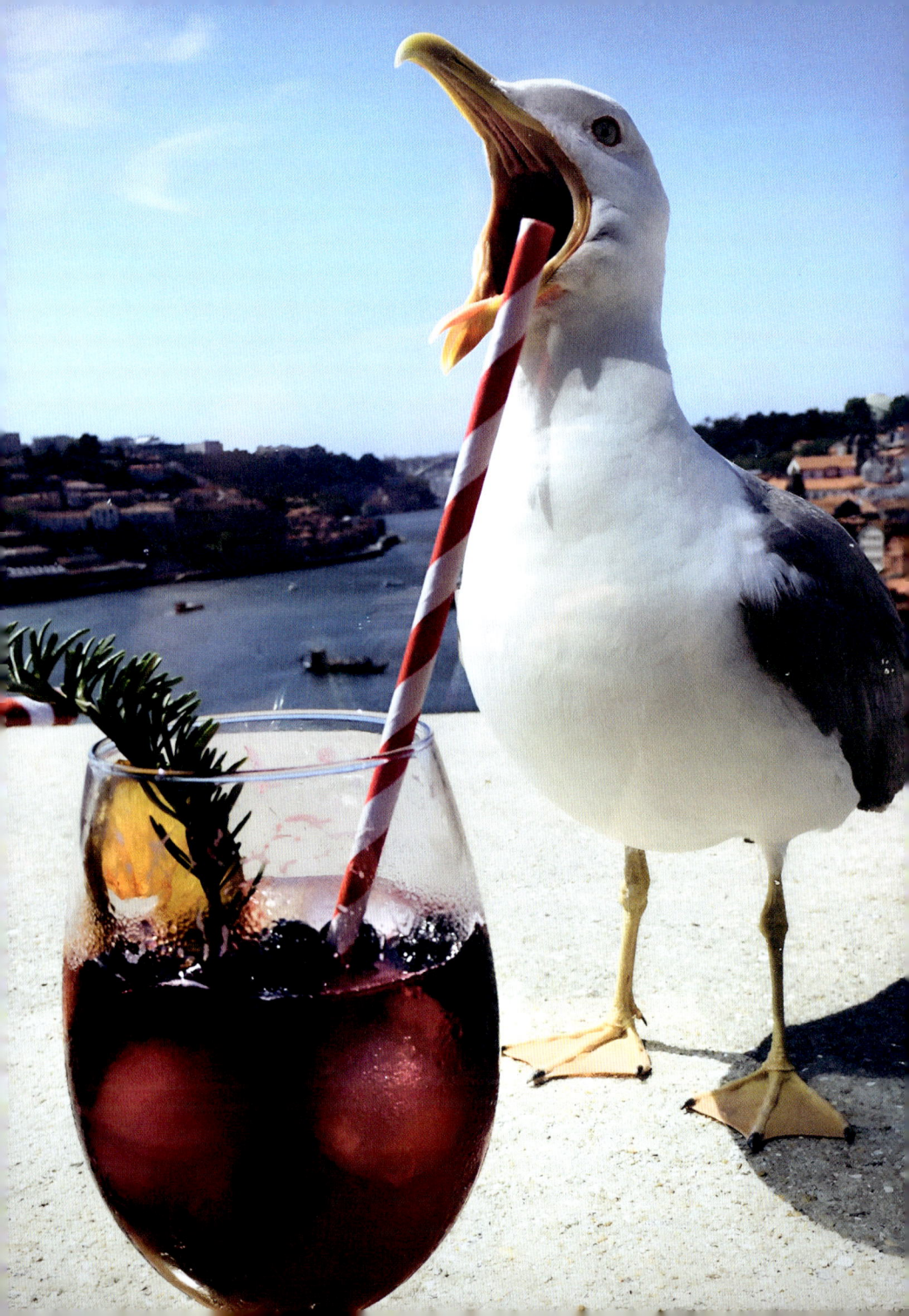

39. HAVE FUN

HUMOUR IS A powerful tool that is difficult to master. Many situations out on the streets can seem like fun, and that is what many street photographers want to capture. Pictures with an amusing or unexpected detail make people laugh, generate moments of recognition and conversations. But humour is very personal; a picture you think is funny someone else may find incomprehensible, boring, or even malicious. There is no right answer, but common elements include contrasts, the unexpected or juxtaposition. Remember that pictures in which something is coming out of the head of someone, or faces that are replaced by symbols, are considered clichés. Read more about juxtaposition on page 44.

CAPTURE THE HUMOROUS SIDE OF STREET LIFE

40. MAKE IT DIFFICULT

YOU COULD EASILY look for outstanding settings so you can capture moments suitable for the photo books of tomorrow. But it may lead to a sense of despair. Everyone cannot be living in a major city or travel to unusual and exotic places. So why not go for the opposite objective. Look for dullness and go to places that at first appear to lack all visual interest. A backyard, a parking lot or an empty playground. How can you find something interesting there? Also see *Immerse Yourself in the Daily Routine* on page 107.

EXPLORE A SEEMINGLY
UNINTERESTING SETTING
IN TERMS OF MOTIF

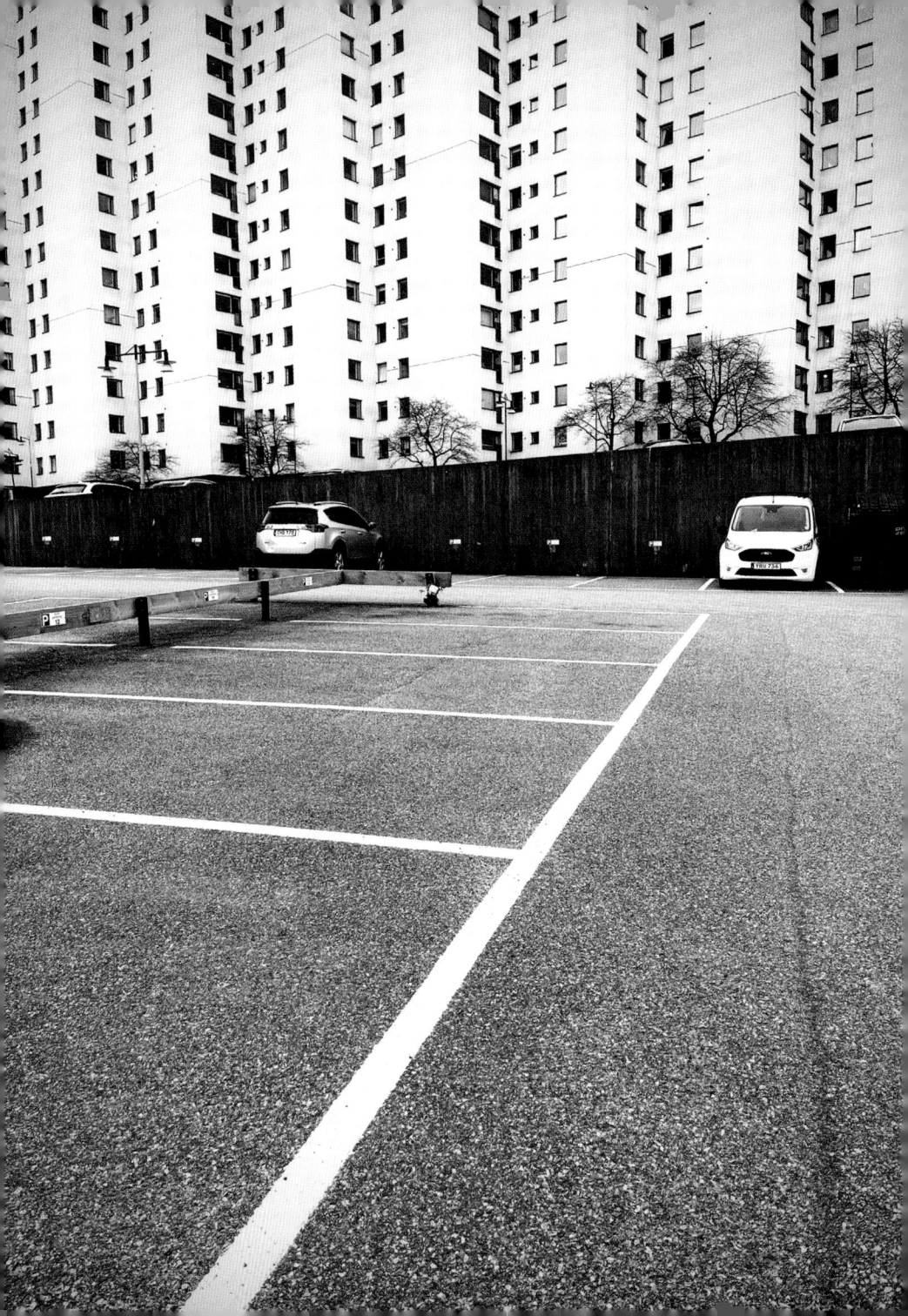

41. PAINT WITH SHADOWS

THE CITY OFFERS a shadow-play of its own. Buildings, vehicles, people or you block out light and create dramatic visual effects. The art of capturing this phenomenon is a highly popular street photography trope. You can create dramatic, magical pictures, frame a subject or capture silhouettes. Of course it matters what time of day you are out. The sharpest contrasts are found at midday. Longer, softer shadows, raking light, appear after sunrise and just before sunset. Backlighting can create reflexes you can use. See also *Follow the Light* on page 58.

MAKE SHADOWS YOUR SUBJECT

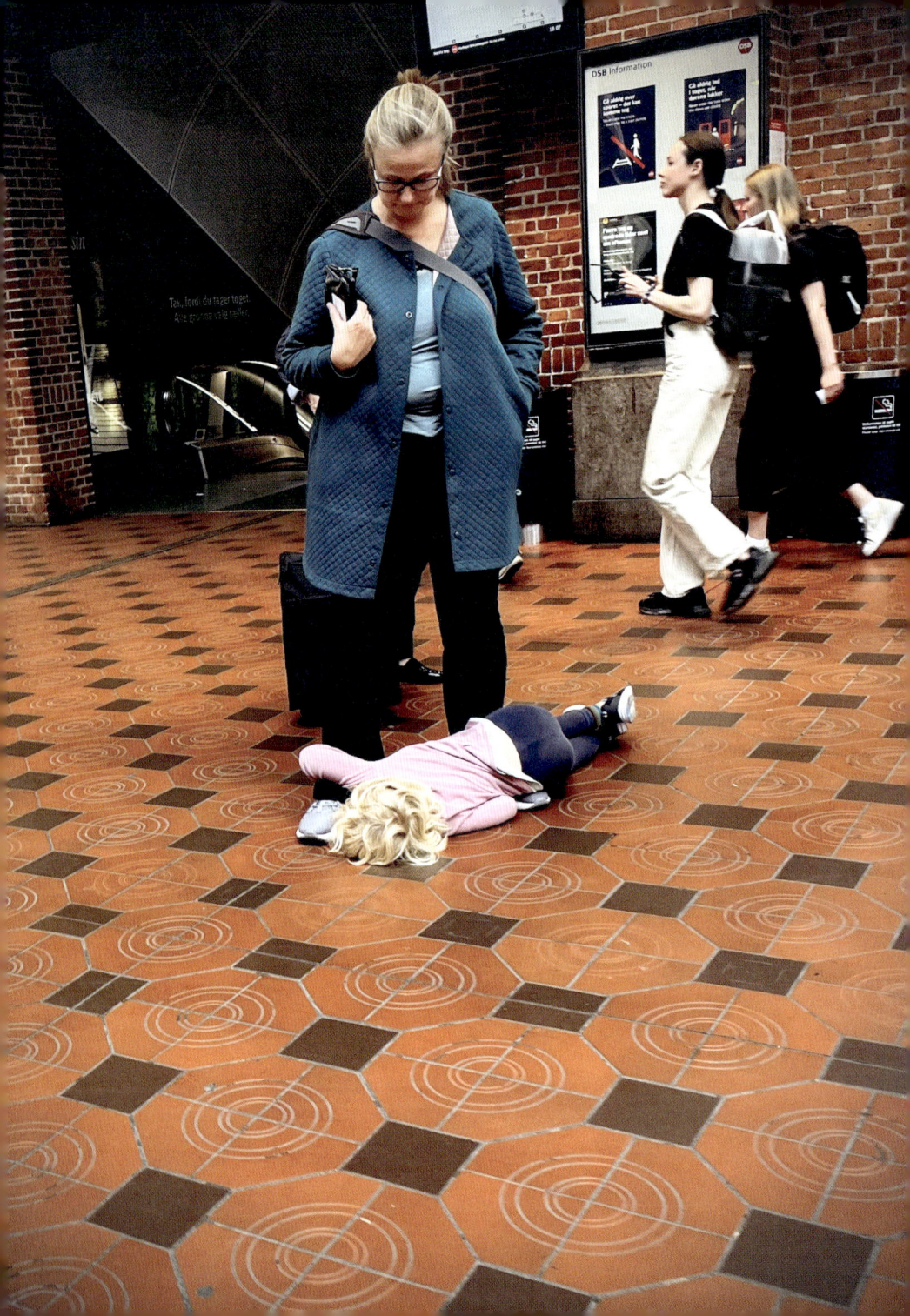

42. IMMERSE YOURSELF IN THE DAILY ROUTINE

WITHIN STREET PHOTOGRAPHY, unique moments and the art of being at the right place at the right time, what Henri Cartier-Bresson has called "the decisive moment", is often highly praised. But it can be just as interesting to document what goes on around us all the time, the ordinary life and quiet monotony. Anything conventional and seemingly banal can be transformed into something surrealist and absurd. Inspiration: Lars Tunbjörk.

DOCUMENT SOMETHING ORDINARY

43. DISCOVER UNEXPECTED PATTERNS

STREET LIFE OFFERS many unexpected shapes and forms, random patterns that appear for a short moment without any human intervention. Suddenly trash, twigs and colour stains become artworks in their own right.

SEARCH THE CITY'S UNEXPECTED PATTERNS

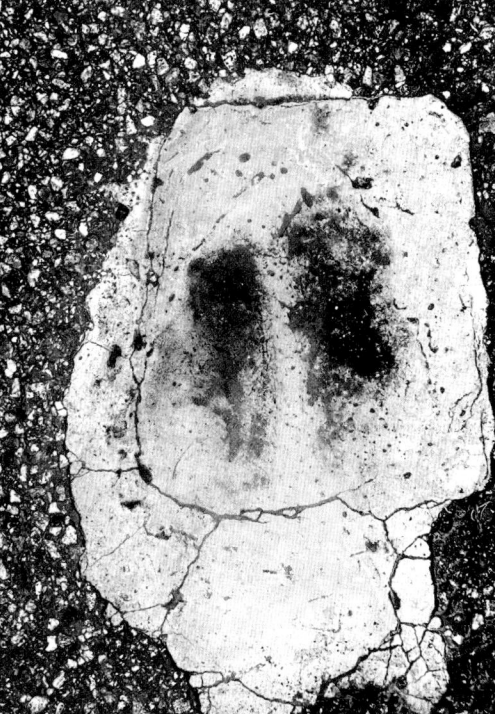

44. CAPTURE COLOURS

WHEN YOU PHOTOGRAPH in colour, the city offers a rich palette that you can use in any number of ways. One is to work with the primary colours blue, yellow and red. They are distinct, eye-catching and sometimes described as "red shirt photography". You can also look for midtones and complementary colours. They are more discreet and are easily found. At night, street lights and neon signs offer exciting displays of colour. See also *Become a Nocturnal Animal* on page 71.

CAPTURE THE COLOURS OF THE RAINBOW, ONE AT A TIME. START WITH RED OR YELLOW, OR _____

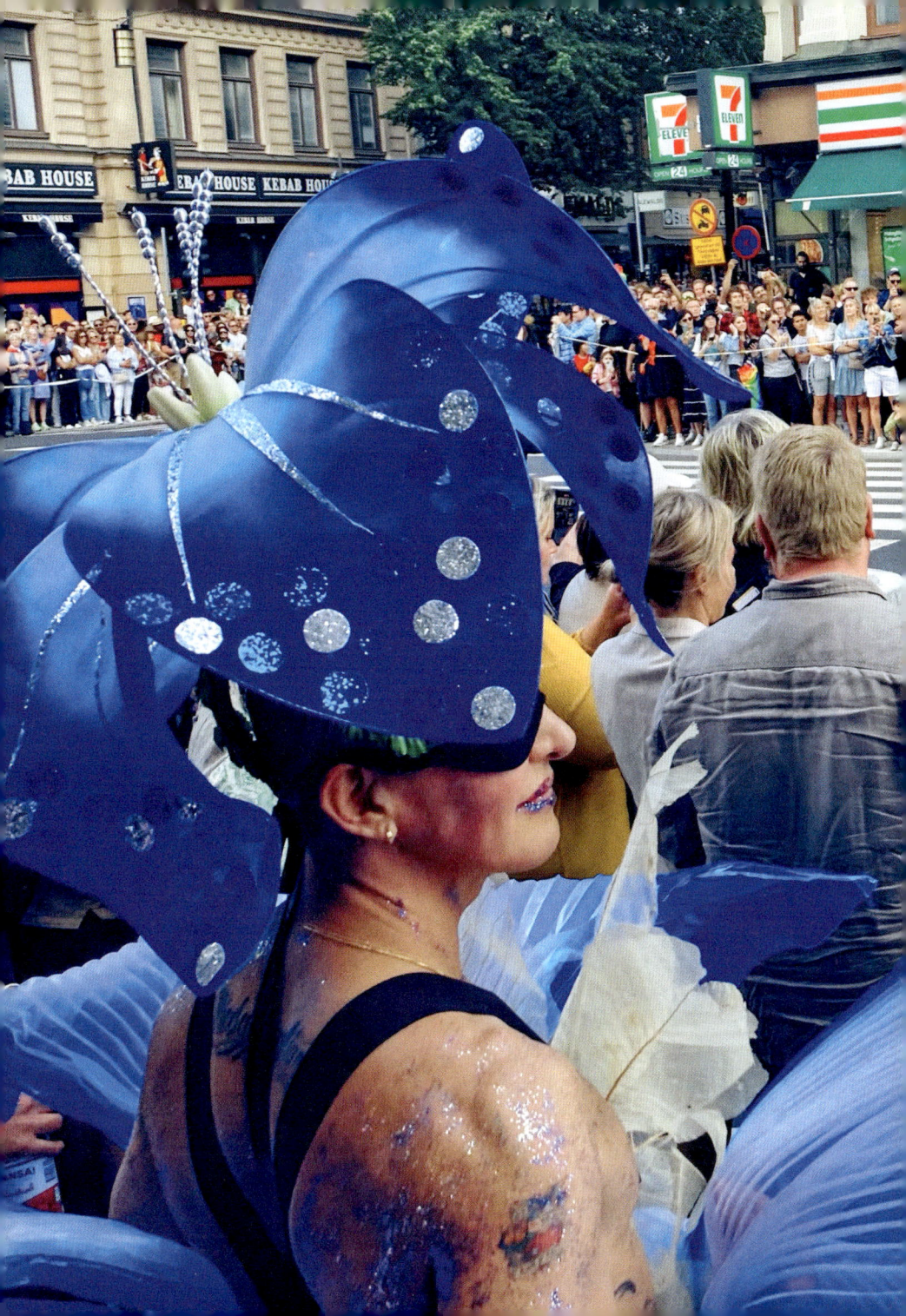

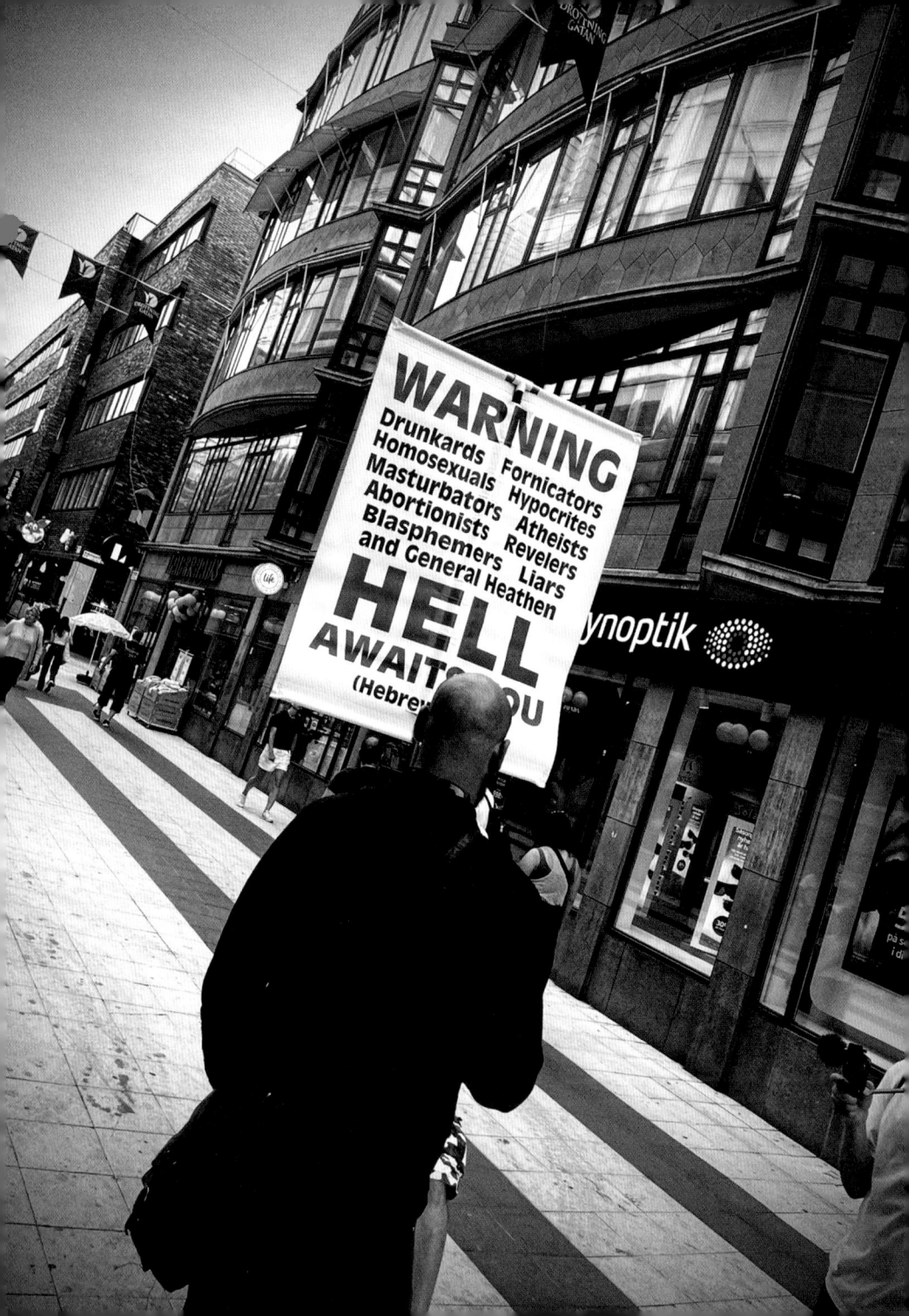

45. SIGNS IN THE CITY

IN THE CITY, information is communicated in many different shapes and styles. Most visible are the letters, numbers and symbols we encounter via advertising, graffiti, street and shop signs. Street photographers can use these as focal points, complements, reliefs or as a background. For many years, Lee Friedlander photographed signs in American cities, thereby offering us a fascinating insight into the way lettering and typography contribute to changing the urban landscape over time.

FOCUS ON THE TYPOGRAPHY
OF THE CITY

46. NO PHOTO DAY

IT IS OFTEN hard to be creative when prompted, and many people claim that the best ideas come to them when they least expect it. The same of course goes for street photography. The best moments do not appear when you think they will. Doing nothing opens up a space for new ideas. According to scientists, boredom makes you more creative, as the brain begins to search for new thoughts, which is a bonus. Make sure to be bored from time to time. And try to leave the camera behind next time you leave home.

*I'M A BIG BELIEVER IN BOREDOM.
BOREDOM ALLOWS ONE TO INDULGE IN CURIOSITY,
AND OUT OF CURIOSITY COMES EVERYTHING.*

Steve Jobs

RELAX. READ A BOOK.

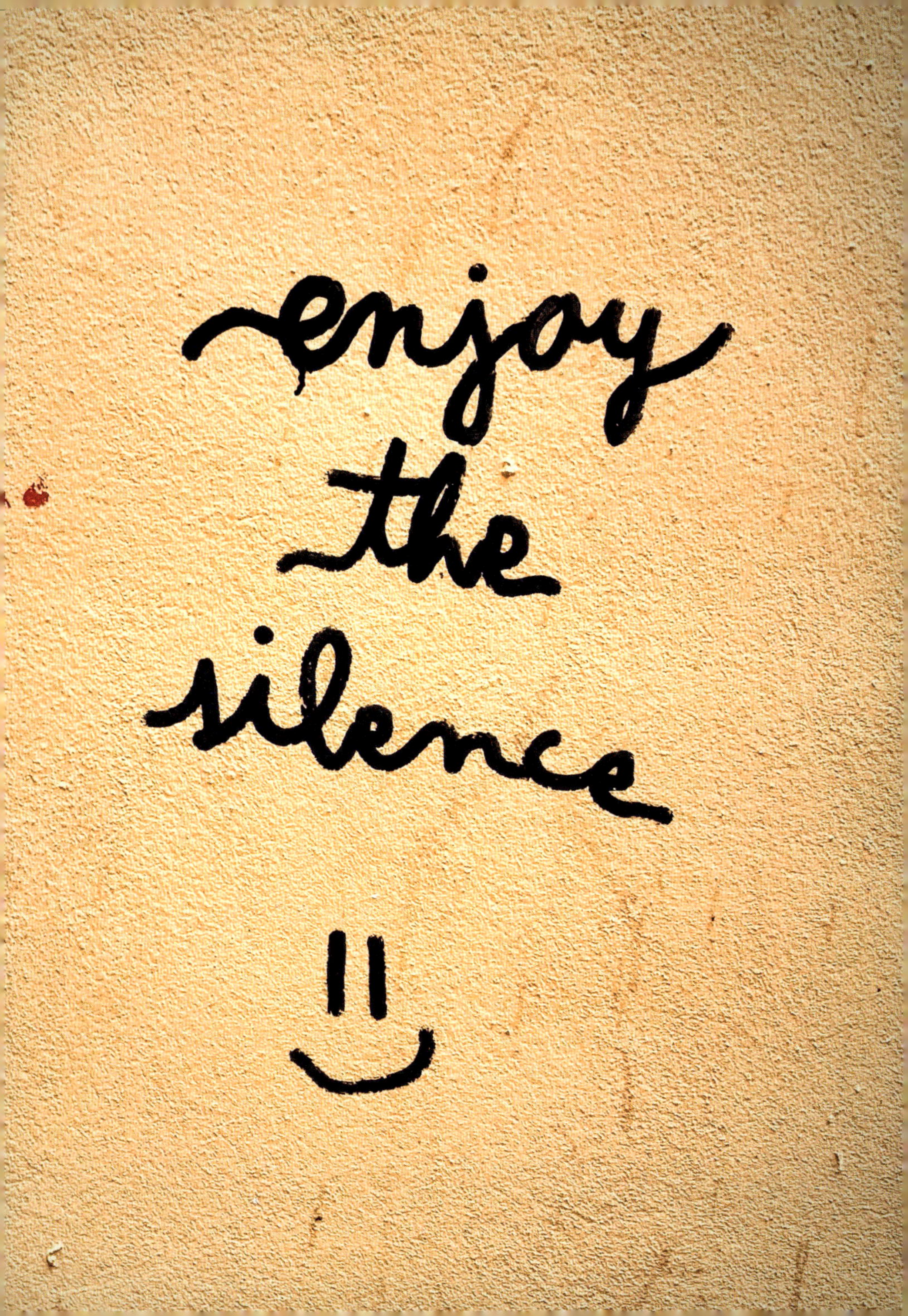
enjoy
the
silence

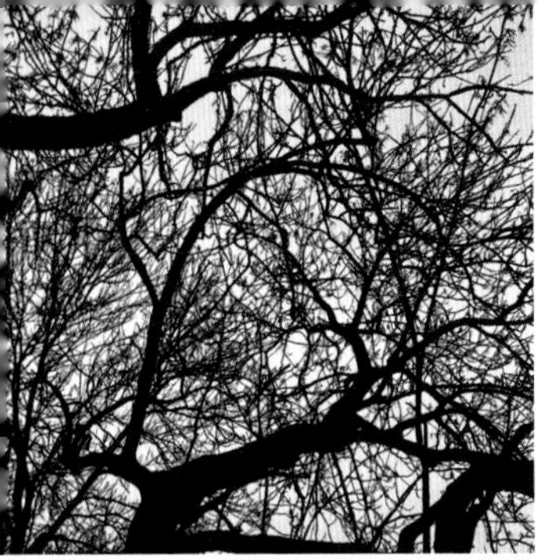

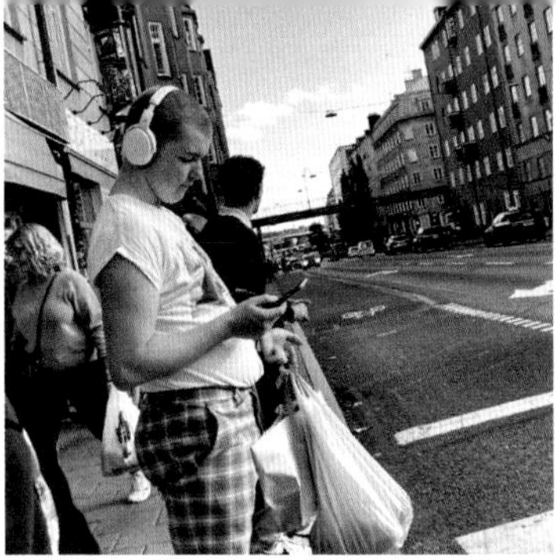

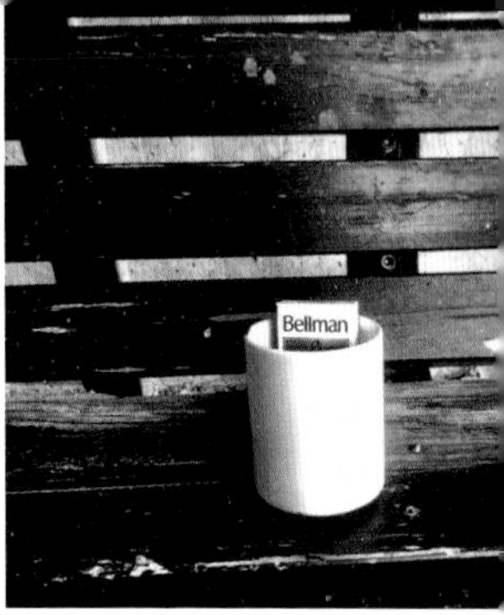

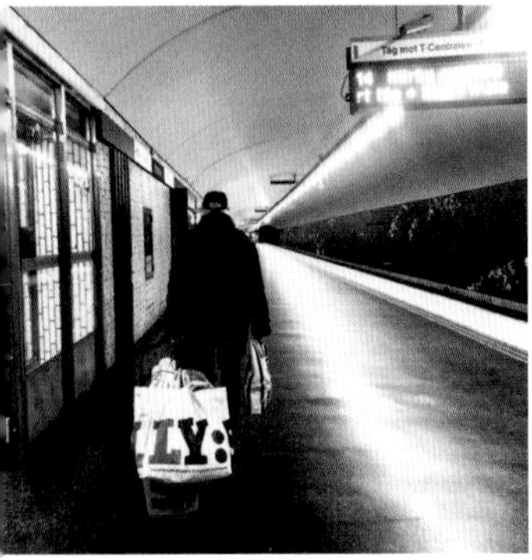

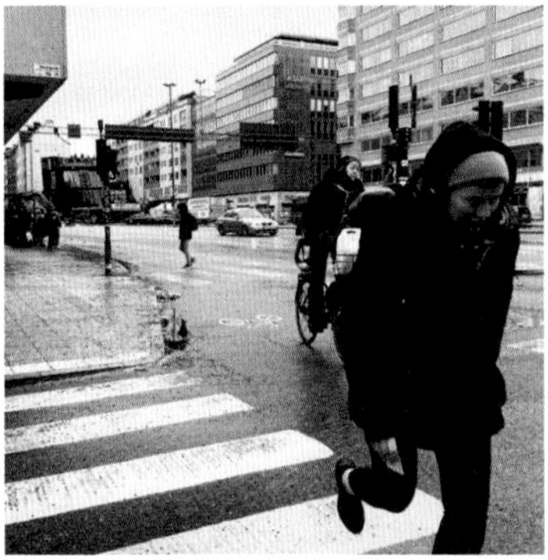

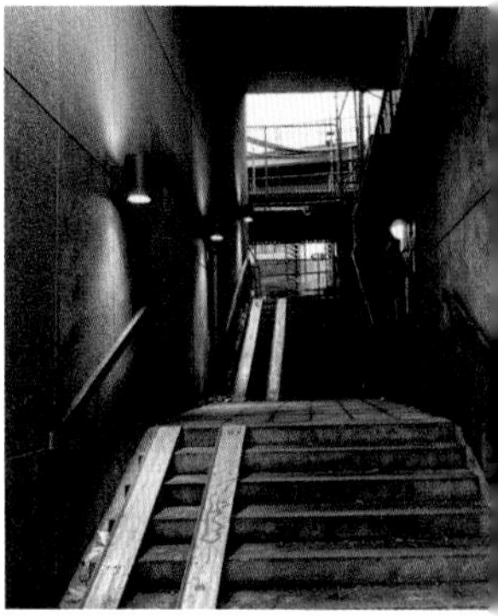

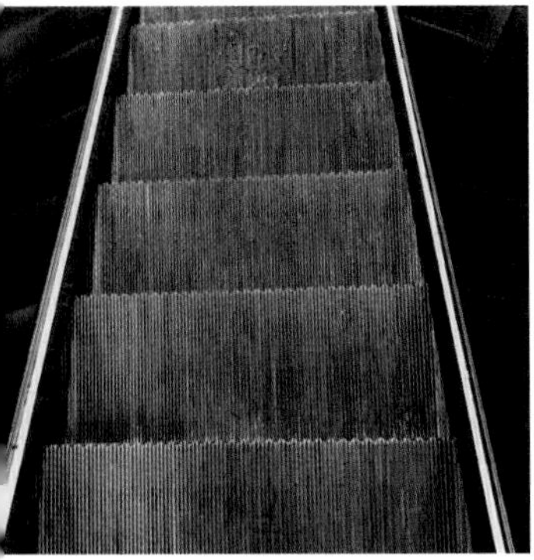

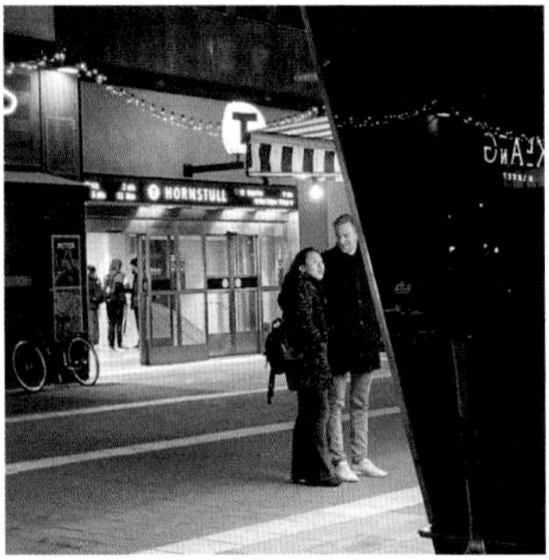

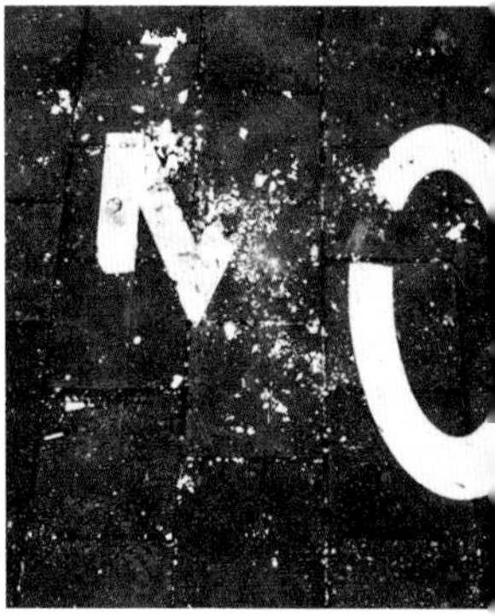

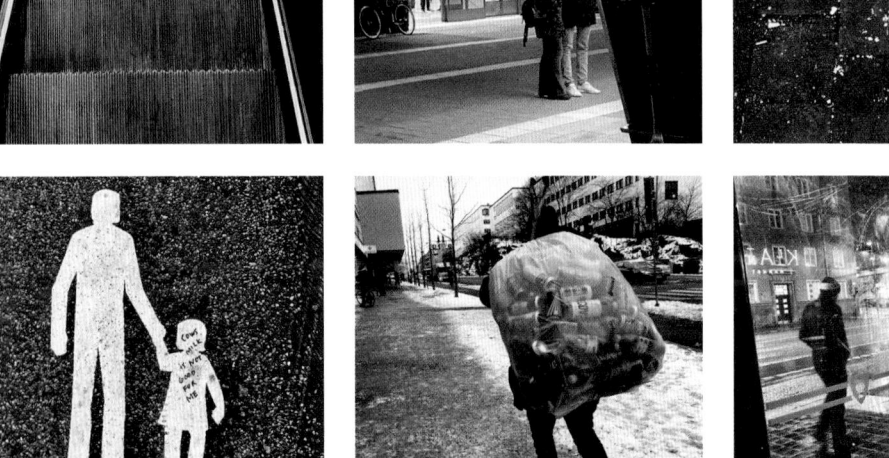

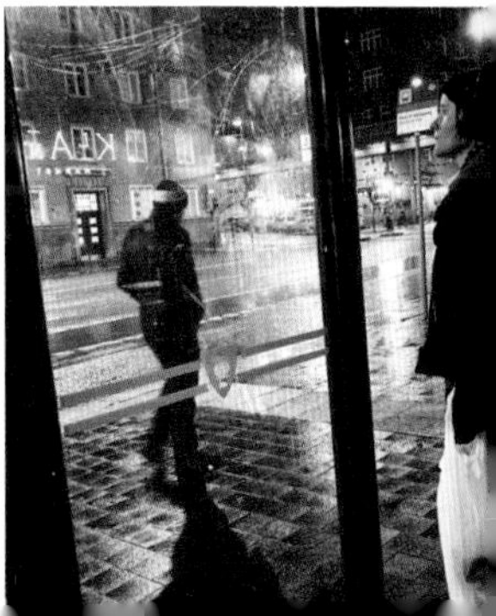

47. A THOUSAND PICTURES

TRY AND TAKE a lot of pictures during a set period of time. Choose one motif and photograph it from as many perspectives and angles as you can think of. Now you have plenty of material to bring back home. Take it easy for a day or two, then sit down in peace and quiet and go through the material. What came out the way you expected? What was unexpected? What can you learn from this method? Choose the 10 best pictures and put them in sequence. See also *Kill Your Darlings* on page 85.

TAKE AS MANY PICTURES AS YOU CAN IN ONE HOUR

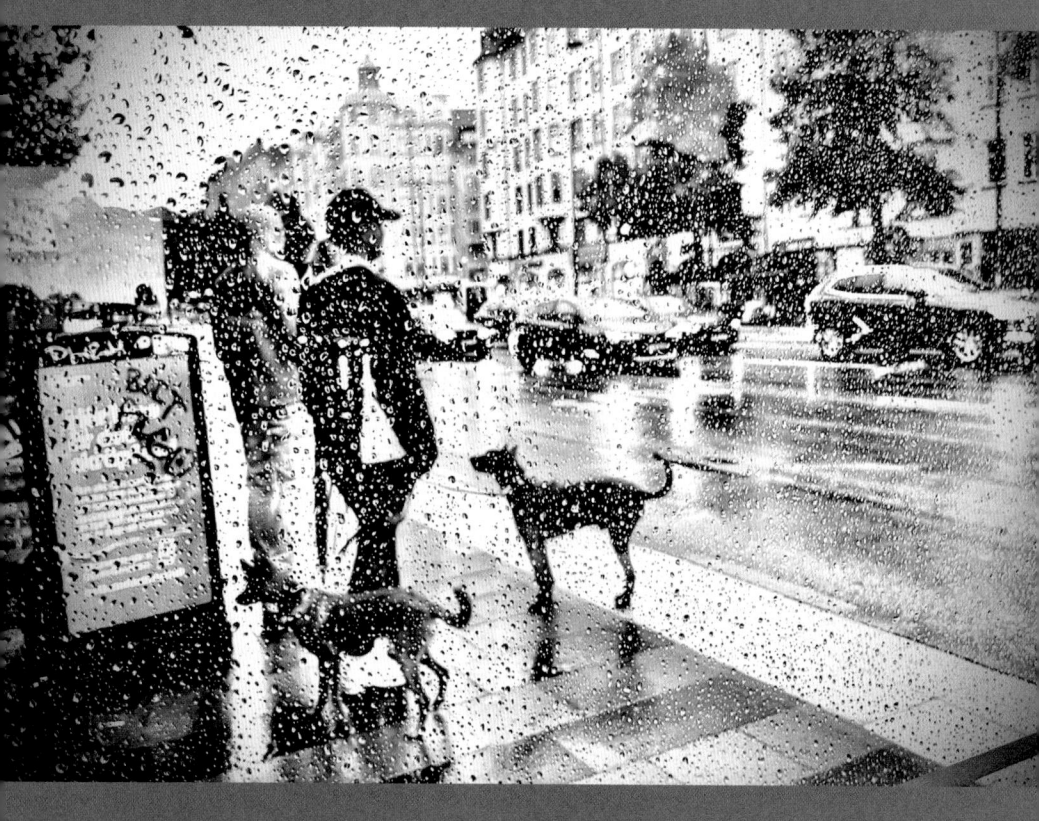

48. THROUGH THE WINDOW

TAKING PICTURES THROUGH glass is a fun and creative challenge. Windows can become filters that create distance. They can also offer strong visual effects in the form of refraction and multidimensional imagery. Colours distort, mirror images and reflections appear. The latter is popular among many street photographers and has become a distinct style within abstract street photography. One, or more, windows can add to a composition by framing subjects. What to consider:

1) Some think that photographing through (bus) windows is a cliché.
2) There is a risk that you disturb people who want to be left in peace.

See also *Be Abstract* on page 75.

49. CLICHÉS?

LIKE ANY OTHER creative activity, there are stereotypes within street photography. Some motifs are so overused that they are considered predictable and unoriginal. Some of the most common include:

- Homeless people out of context
- Overuse of window reflections, mirrors or water puddles
- People standing in front of signs and advertisements
- People photographed from behind
- Street artists and vendors
- People on a long escalator

The cliché debate is not straightforward; there are many opinions and a lot of lecturing. While being aware of it, you should not take too much notice of other people's opinions. See also *Kill Your Darlings* on page 85 and *Get to Know Your Prejudices* on page 60.

DELIBERATELY USE SOME STREET PHOTOGRAPHY CLICHÉS

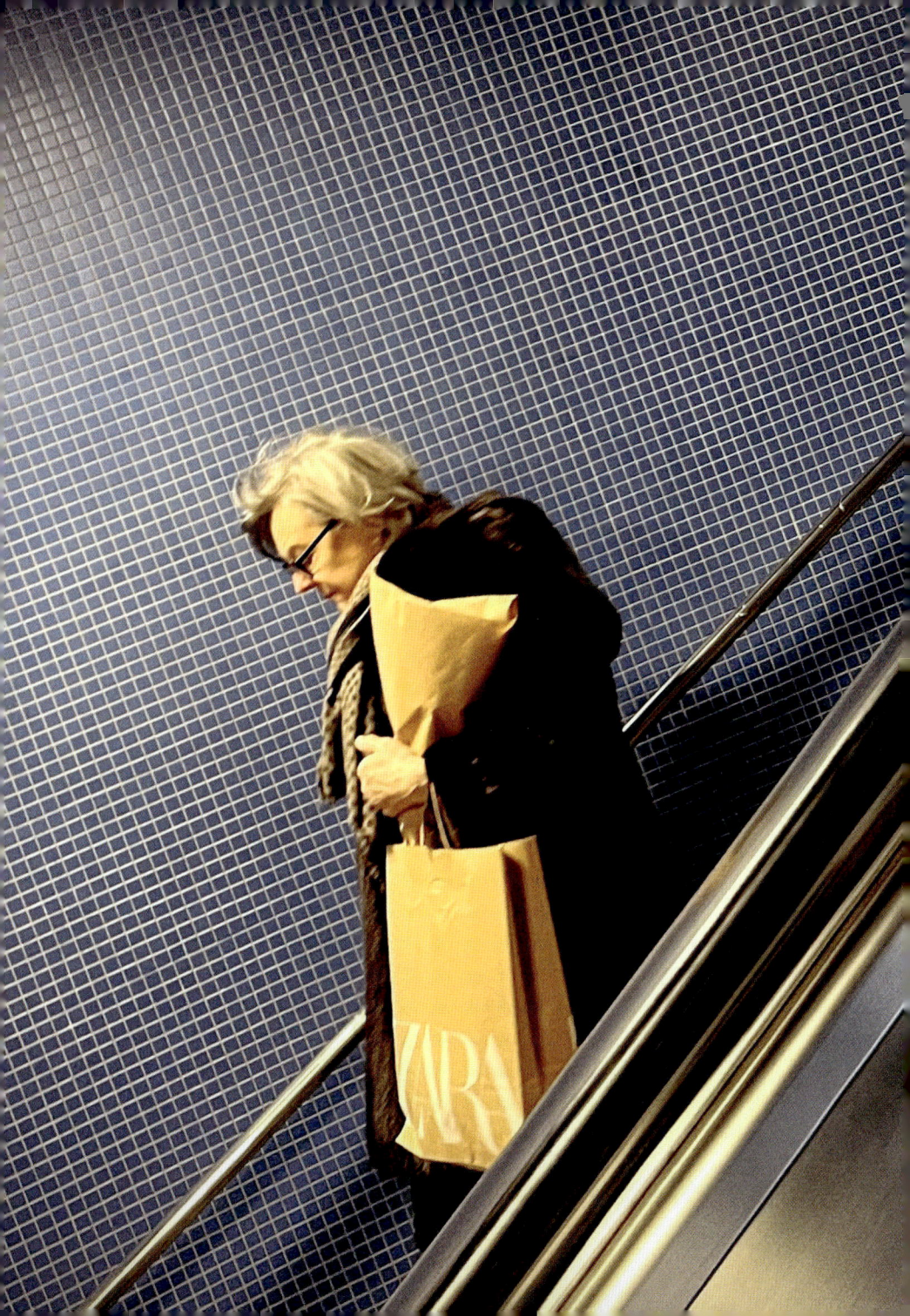

50. ILLUSTRATE SOMETHING

STREET PHOTOGRAPHERS TEND to wait for something to happen. This time, try and look for a motif to illustrate an idea. An image that will symbolize a vision or concept you want to present. How can street life serve to illustrate your interpretation of a favourite book, or a film you saw recently? One genre that is similar to this is cinematic street photography, where you look for street life that resembles scenes from a film.

TAKE A PICTURE FOR A BOOK
COVER OR A FILM POSTER

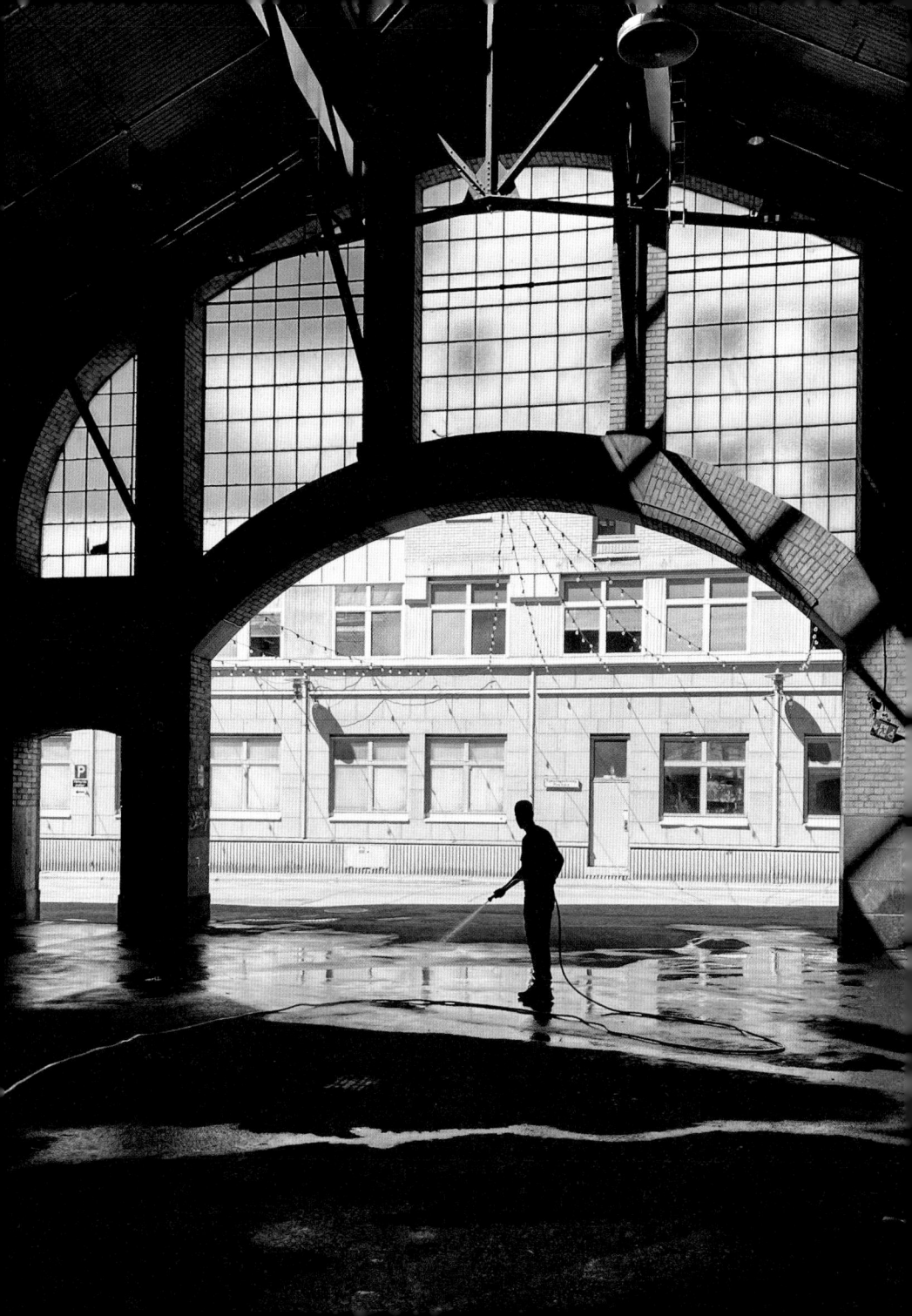

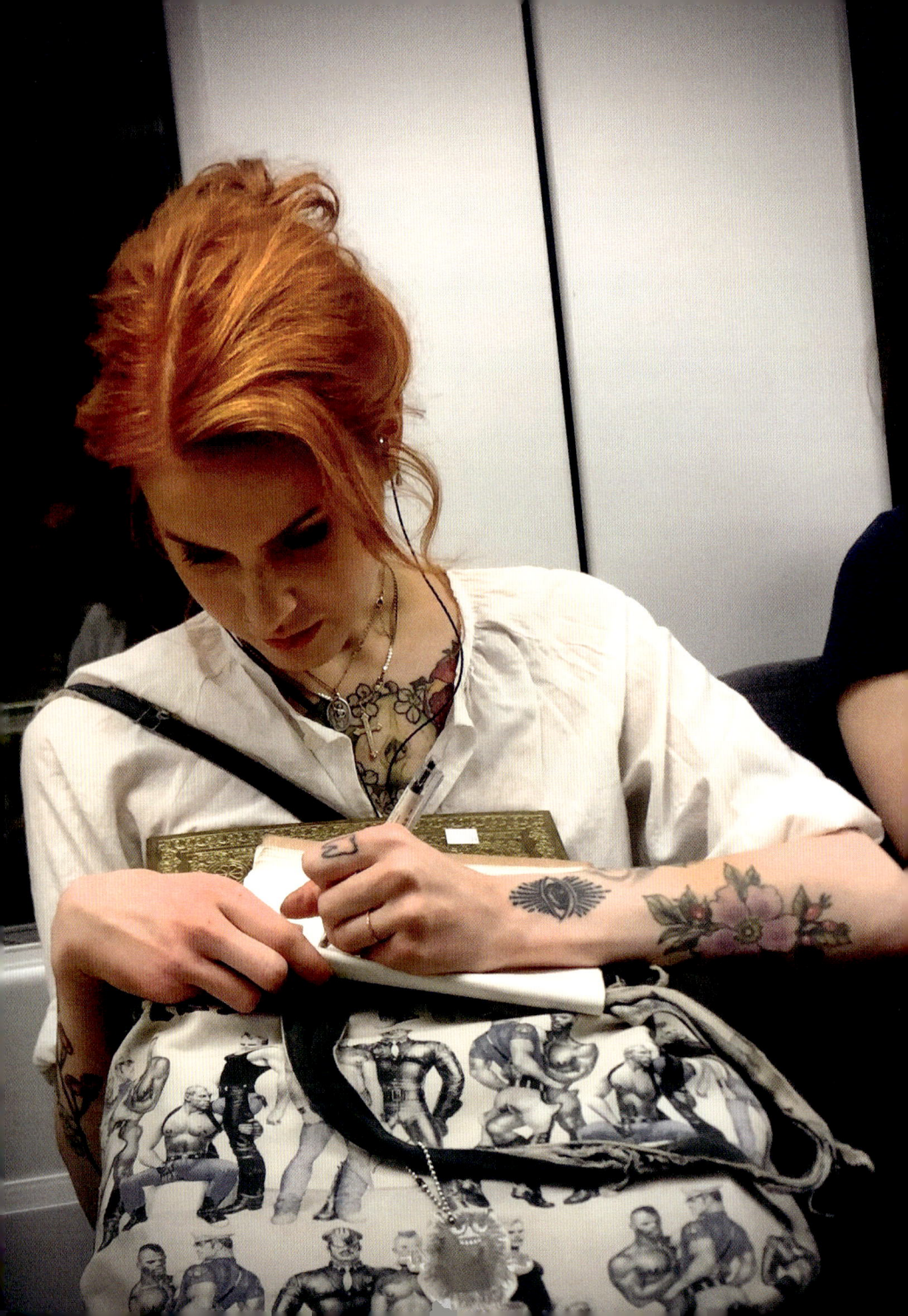

WHEN YOU THOUGHT YOU HAD DONE IT ALL

HAVE YOU DONE all the challenges mentioned in this book? Then try some of these. Photograph:

- Stress – People in a hurry
- Examples of gentrification
- Lunch – People who eat fast food
- The moment it starts to rain
- A profession
- Hands that are doing something
- Only black and white
- Someone on public transport who is not using a mobile phone
- Emotions: anger, joy or weariness
- Life at a bus stop
- People wearing baseball caps
- Shoes
- While you're running
- From the roof of a building
- Only motifs that are exactly one metre away

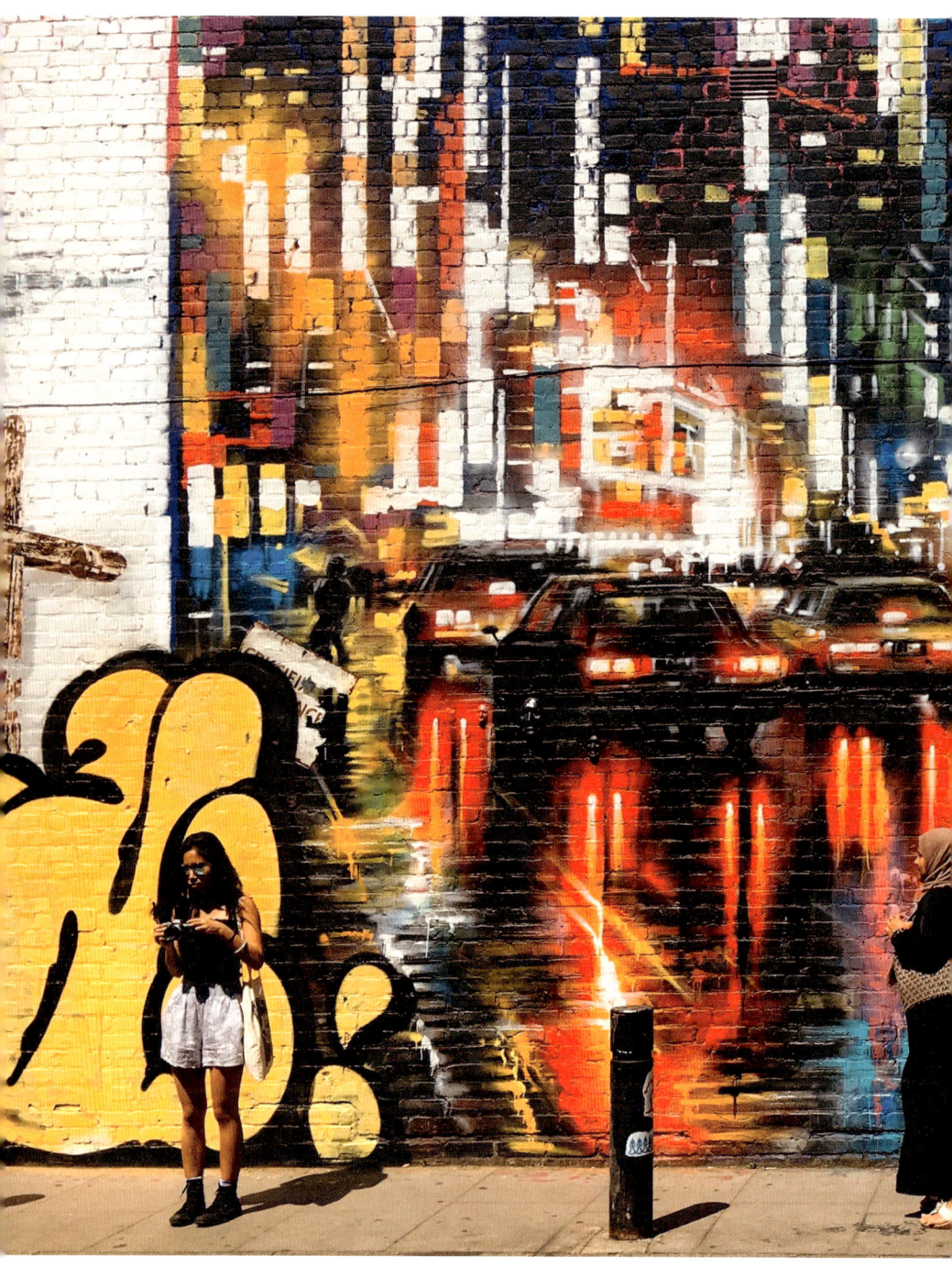

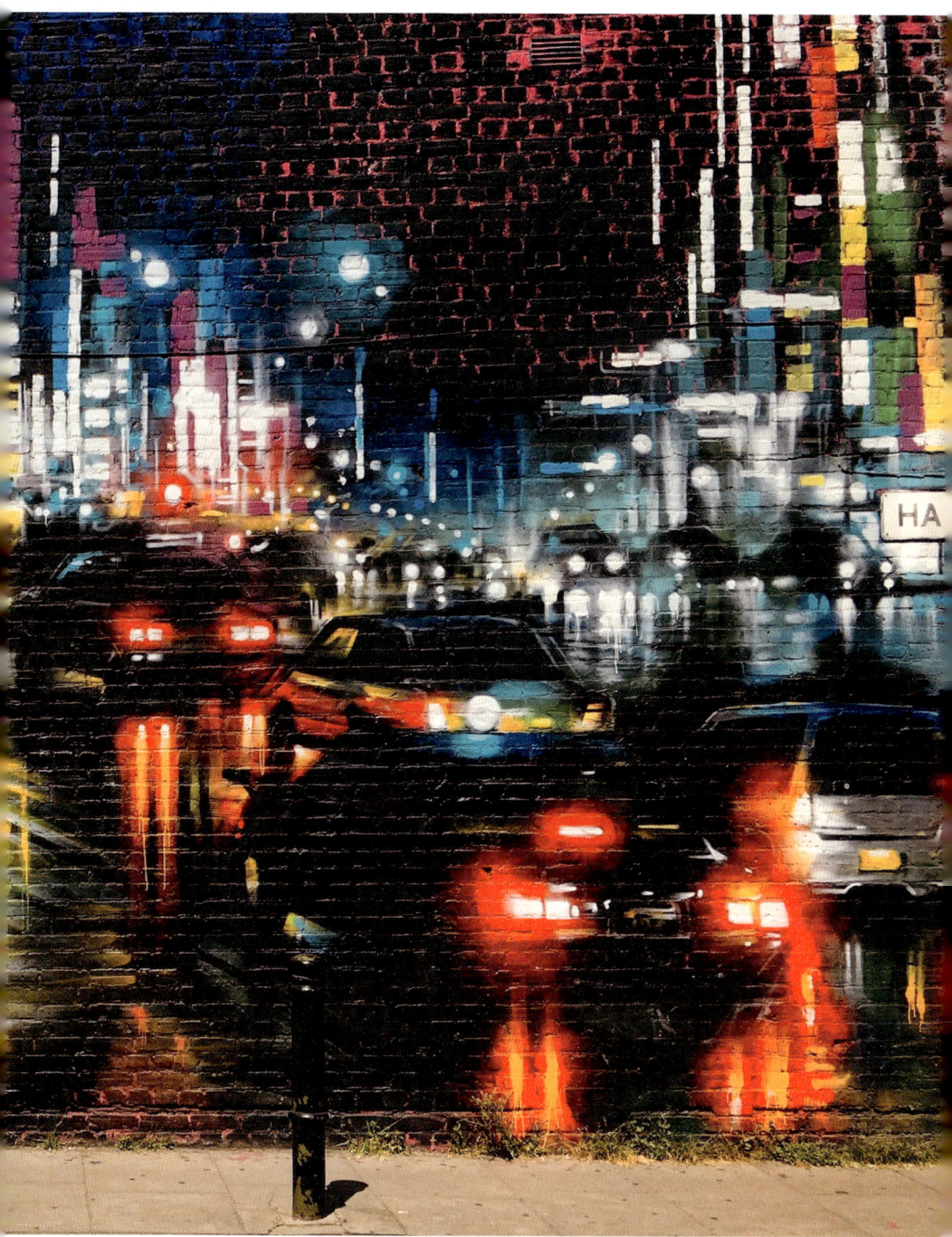

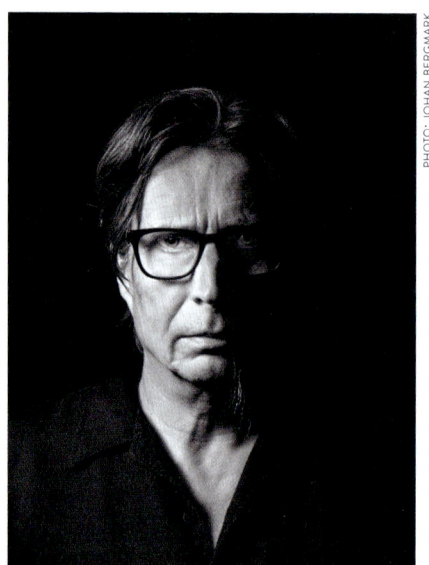

BENKE CARLSSON is a photographer and writer living in Stockholm, Sweden. He is the author of the books *Street Art Stockholm*, *Street Art Cookbook* and *Swedish Punk 1977–81* and runs a small gallery (C/O Hornstull) and Bly Publishing. Benke also works as head of strategy at OTW Communication and is a well-renowned consultant on branding, communication, and art. The photographs in this book were spontaneously taken with a smartphone, many of them in the streets around Hornstull in Stockholm and during trips to cities such as Addis Ababa, Buenos Aires, Copenhagen, Gothenburg, Helsinki, Lisbon, London, Madrid, Malmö, New York, Nice, Porto, San Sebastian, and São Paulo.